A
COMPACT
ANTHOLOGY
OF
BARTLETT'S
QUOTATIONS

Compiled and Arranged
by
Theodore B. Backer

JONATHAN DAVID PUBLISHERS
MIDDLE VILLAGE, N. Y. 11379

A COMPACT ANTHOLOGY
OF
BARTLETT'S QUOTATIONS
by
Theodore B. Backer

Copyright © 1974
by
Jonathan David Publishers

JONATHAN DAVID PUBLISHERS
68-22 Eliot Avenue
Middle Village, New York 11379

PRINTED IN THE UNITED STATES OF AMERICA

Library of Congress Cataloging in Publication Data

Bartlett, John, 1820-1905, comp.
  A compact anthology of Bartlett's quotations.

  1. Quotations, English. I. Backer, Theodore B.,
1940- ed. II. Title.
PN6081.B27 1974   808.88'2   74-1964
ISBN 0-8246-0178-X

A COMPACT ANTHOLOGY
OF
BARTLETT'S QUOTATIONS

HOMER
(Circa 850 B.C.)

Words sweet as honey from his lips distill'd.

Iliad. Book I, Line 332

The man who acts the least, upbraids the most.

Iliad. Book II, Line 311

But when he speaks, what elocution flows!
Soft as the fleeces of descending snows
The copious accents fall, with easy art;
Melting they fall, and sink into the heart.

Iliad. Book III, Line 283

Like leaves on trees the race of man is found,
Now green in youth, now withering on the ground:
Another race the following spring supplies:
They fall successive, and successive rise.

Iliad. Book VI, Line 181

He serves me most, who serves his country best.

Iliad. Book X, Line 201

No season now for calm, familiar talk,
Like youths and maidens in an evening walk.

Iliad. Book XXII, Line 169

Achilles absent was Achilles still.

Iliad. Book XXII, Line 418

HESIOD
(Circa 720 B.C.?)

A bad neighbour is as great a misfourtune as a good one is a great blessing.

Works and Days, Line 346

1

If thou shouldst lay up even a little upon a little, and shouldst do this often, soon would even this become great.

Works and Days, Line 360

Neither make thy friend equal to a brother; but if thou shalt have made him so, be not the first to do him wrong.

Works and Days, Line 707

SOLON
(638?-559 B.C.)

I grow old learning something new every day.

Valerius Maximus: Book VIII, Chap. 7, Sect. 14

SAPPHO OF LESBOS
(Circa 610 B.C.)

Art thou the topmost apple
The gatherers could not reach,
Reddening on the bough?

To Atthis, paraphrase by Bliss Carman

AESOP
(Floruit 550 B.C.)

Any excuse will serve a tyrant.

The Wolf and the Lamb

Beware lest you lose the substance by grasping at the shadow.

The Dog and the Shadow

You may share the labours of the great, but you will not share the spoil.

The Lion's Share

You have put your head inside a wolf's mouth and taken it out again in safety. That ought to be reward enough for you.

The Wolf and the Crane

Better beans and bacon in peace than cakes and ale in fear.

The Town Mouse and the Country Mouse

Only cowards insult dying majesty.

The Sick Lion

Little friends may prove great friends.

> *The Lion and the Mouse*

Better no rule than cruel rule.

> *The Frogs Desiring a King*

Much outcry, little outcome.

> *The Mountains in Labour*

There is always someone worse off than yourself.

> *The Hares and the Frogs*

It is easy to be brave from a safe distance.

> *The Wolf and the Kid*

Outside show is a poor substitute for inner worth.

> *The Fox and the Mask*

It is not only fine feathers that make fine birds.

> *The Jay and the Peacock*

Self-conceit may lead to self-destruction.

> *The Frog and the Ox*

Gratitude is the sign of noble souls.

> *Androcles*

We often despise what is most useful to us.

> *The Hart and the Hunter*

They found that even the Belly, in its dull quiet way, was doing necessary work for the Body, and that all must work together or the Body will go to pieces.

> *The Belly and the Members*

It is easy to despise what you cannot get.

> *The Fox and the Grapes*

Be content with your lot; one cannot be first in everything.

> *The Peacock and Juno*

Familiarity breeds contempt.

> *The Fox and the Lion*

The Lamb that belonged to the Sheep, whose skin the Wolf was wearing, began to follow the Wolf in the Sheep's clothing.

> *The Wolf in Sheep's Clothing*

Appearances are deceptive.

> *The Wolf in Sheep's Clothing*

The boy called out "Wolf, Wolf!" and the villagers came out to help him. A few days afterward he tried the same trick, and again they came to his help. Shortly after this a Wolf actually came, but this time the villagers thought the boy was deceiving them again and nobody came to his help.

The Shepherd's Boy

A liar will not be believed, even when he speaks the truth.

The Shepherd's Boy

United we stand, divided we fall.

The Four Oxen and the Lion

A little thing in hand is worth more than a great thing in prospect.

The Fisher and the Little Fish

Little by little does the trick.

The Crow and the Pitcher

I will have nought to do with a man who can blow hot and cold with the same breath.

The Man and the Satyr

When the Hare awoke from his nap, he saw the Tortoise just near the winning post. Plodding wins the race.

The Hare and the Tortoise

Union gives strength.

The Bundle of Sticks

Do not count your chickens before they are hatched.

The Milkmaid and Her Pail

AESCHYLUS
(525-456 B.C.)

I think the slain
Care little if they sleep or rise again;
And we, the living, wherefore should we ache
With counting all our lost ones?

Agamemnon, Line 595

Sweet is a grief well ended.

Agamemnon, Line 805

For not many men, the proverb saith,
Can love a friend whom fortune prospereth
Unenvying.

Agamemnon, Line 832

I know how men in exile feed on dreams.

Agamemnon, Line 1668

God lives to help him who strives to help himself.

Fragment 223

PINDAR
(522-422 B.C.)

We are creatures of a day. What is one, what is one not? Man is a dream of a shadow.

Pythian Ode 8

SOPHOCLES
(496?-406 B.C.)

None love the messenger who brings bad news.

Antigone

For money you would sell your soul.

Antigone

There lives no greater fiend than Anarchy;
She ruins states, turns houses out of doors,
Breaks up in rout the embattled soldiery.

Antigone

Wonders are many, and none is more wonderful than man.

Antigone

Though a man be wise
It is no shame for him to live and learn.

Antigone

To err
From the right path is common to mankind.

Antigone

A woman should be seen, not heard.

Ajax

I for my own part, having learnt of late
Those hateful to us we are not to hate
As though they might not soon be friends again,
Intend to measure, now, the services
I render to my friend, as if not so
To abide for ever; for of mortals most
Find friendship an unstable anchorage.

Ajax

Never to have been born is much the best;
And the next best, by far,
To return thence, by the way speediest,
Where our beginnings are.

Oedipus Coloneius

If I am Sophocles, I am not mad; and if I am mad, I am not Sophocles.

Vita Anonyma

EURIPIDES
(484-406 B.C.)

I care for riches, to make gifts
To friends, or lead a sick man back to health
With ease and plenty. Else small aid is wealth
For daily gladness; once a man be done
With hunger, rich and poor are all as one.

Electra. Line 539

Moderation, the noblest gift of Heaven.

Medea. Line 636

The company of just and righteous men is better than wealth and a rich estate.

Aegeus. Fragment 7

HERODOTUS
(484-424 B.C.)

A man trusts his ears less than his eyes.

Book I, Clio. Chap. 8

Call no man happy till you know the nature of his death; he is at best but fortunate.

Book I, Clio. Chap. 32

How much better it is to be envied than pitied.

Book III, Thalia. Chap. 52

Envy is natural to man from the beginning.

Book III, Thalia. Chap 80

THUCYDIDES
(471-401 B.C.)

Of the events of war, I have not ventured to speak from any chance information, nor according to any notion of my own; I have described nothing but what I saw myself, or learned from others of whom I made the most careful and particular inquiry. The task was a laborious one because eyewitnesses of the same occurrence gave different accounts of them as they remembered, or were interested in the actions of one side or the other. And very likely the strictly historical character of my narrative may be disappointing to the ear. But if he who desires to have before his eyes a true picture of the events which have happened, and of the like events which may be expected to happen hereafter in the order of human things, shall pronounce what I have written to be useful, then I shall be satisfied. My history is an everlasting possession, not a prize composition which is heard and forgotten.

Peloponnesian War. Book I

Mankind is tolerant of the praises of others so long as each hearer thinks he can do as well or nearly as well himself, but, when the speaker rises above him, jealousy is aroused and he begins to be incredulous.

Peloponnesian War. Book II, 35
Funeral Speech of Pericles

SOCRATES
(470-399 B.C.)

The life which is unexamined is not worth living.

Apology 38

Man is a prisoner who has no right to open the door of his prison and run away ... A man should wait, and not take his own life until God summons him.

Dialogues of Plato. Phaedo 62

False words are not only evil in themselves, but they infect the soul with evil.

Dialogues of Plato. Phaedo 62

HIPPOCRATES
(460-377 B.C.)

I swear by Apollo Physician, by Asclepius, by Health, by Panacea, and by all the gods and goddesses making them my witnesses, that I will carry out, according to my ability and judgment, this oath and this indenture. To hold my teacher in this art equal to my own parents; to make him partner in my livelihood; when he is in need of money to share mine with him; to consider his family as my own brothers, and to teach them this art, if they want to learn it, without fee or indenture. I will use treatment to help the sick according to my ability and judgment, but never with a view to injury and wrongdoing. I will keep pure and holy both my life and my art. In whatsoever houses I enter, I will enter to help the sick, and I will abstain from all intentional wrongdoing and harm. And whatsoever I shall see or hear in the course of my profession in my intercourse with men, if it be what should not be published abroad, I will never divulge, holding such things to be holy secrets. Now if I carry out this oath, and break it not, may I gain forever reputation among all men for my life and for my art; but if I transgress it and forswear myself, may the opposite befall me.

The Physician's Oath

PLATO
(427-347 B.C.)

He who is of a calm and happy nature will hardly feel the pressure of age, but to him who is of an opposite disposition youth and age are equally a burden.

The Republic. Book I, 329-D

Necessity, who is the mother of invention.
The Republic. Book II, 369-C

The beginning is the most important part of the work.
The Republic. 377-B

Musical training is a more potent instrument than any other, because rhythm and harmony find their way into the inward places of the soul.
The Republic. 401-D

Gymnastic as well as music should begin in early years.
The Republic. 403-C

Oligarchy: A government resting on a valuation of property, in which the rich have power and the poor man is deprived of it.
The Republic. Book VIII, 550-C

Democracy, which is a charming form of government, full of variety and disorder, and dispensing a sort of equality to equals and unequals alike.
The Republic. 558-C

You are young, my son, and, as the years go by, time will change and even reverse many of your present opinions. Refrain therefore awhile from setting yourself up as a judge of the highest matter.
Laws 888

ARISTOTLE
(384-322 B.C.)

Poverty is the parent of revolution and crime.
Politics. Book II

Even when laws have been written down, they ought not always to remain unaltered.
Politics. Book II

If liberty and equality, as is thought by some, are chiefly to be found in democracy, they will be best attained when all persons alike share in the government to the utmost.
Politics. Book IV

The best political community is formed by citizens of the middle class. Those States are likely to be well administered in which the middle class is large, and larger if possible than both the other classes, or at any rate than either singly; for the addition of the middle class turns the scale and prevents either of the extremes from being dominant.

Politics

One swallow does not make a spring.

Nicomachean Ethics

Of evils we must choose the least.

Nicomachean Ethics

Misfortune unites men, when the same thing is harmful to both.

Rhetoric I

No one loves him whom he fears.

Rhetoric II

MARCUS TULLIUS CICERO
(106-43 B.C.)

If you aspire to the highest place it is no disgrace to stop at the second, or even the third.

De Oratore

He was never less at leisure than when at leisure.

De Officiis III, quoting
Scipio Africanus

What a time! What a civilization!

Catiline

For how many things, which for our own sake we should never do, do we perform for the sake of our friends.

De Amicitia XVI

When Fortune is fickle, the faithful friend is found.

De Amicitia XVII

For as I like a young man in whom there is something of the old, so I like an old man in whom there is something of the young; and he who follows this maxim, in body will possibly be an old man, but he will never be an old man in mind.

De Senectute XI

VIRGIL
(70-19 B.C.)

Love conquers all.

Eclogues X, Line 69

Not unacquainted with sorrow, I have learned to aid the unfortunate.

Aeneid. Book I, Line 630

A fickle and changeful thing is woman ever.

Aeneid. Book IV, Line 569

HORACE
(65-8 B.C.)

One night waits all; Death's road we all must go.

Odes. Book I, xxviii, Line 16

Spring's flower, howe'er they bloom, must fade again.

Odes. Book II, xi, Line 9

It is sweet and honourable to die for one's country.

Odes. Book III, ii, Line 13

With you I should love to live, with you be ready to die.

Odes. Book III, ix, Line 24

As riches grow, care follows, and a thirst
For more and more.

Odes. Book III, xvi, Line 17

Old men are only walking hospitals.

Ars Poetica. Line 202

Whatever you teach, be brief, that your readers' minds may readily comprehend and faithfully retain your words. Everything superfluous slips from the full heart.

Ars Poetica. Line 335

SENECA
(8 B.C.-A.D. 65)

What fools these mortals be.

Epistles. 1,3

It is not the man who has too little, but the man who craves more, that is poor.

Epistles. 2,2

Live among men as if God beheld you; speak to God as if men were listening.

Epistles. 10,5

Men do not care how nobly they live, but only how long, although it is within the reach of every man to live nobly, but within no man's power to live long.

Epistles. 22,17

It is quality rather than quantity that matters.

Epistles. 45,1

You can tell the character of every man when you see how he receives praise.

Epistles. 52,12

PLINY THE ELDER
(A.D. 23-79)

It is ridiculous to suppose that the great head of things, whatever it be, pays any regard to human affairs.

Natural History. Book I, Sect. 20

Man is the only one that knows nothing, that can learn nothing without being taught. He can neither speak nor walk nor eat, and in short he can do nothing at the prompting of nature only, but weep.

Natural History. Book VII, Sect. 4

PLUTARCH
(A.D. 46-120)

Caesar said he loved the treason, but hated the traitor.

Lives. Romulus. Page 36

Laughing at his own son, who got his mother, and, by his mother's means, his father also, to indulge him, he told him that he had the most power of any one in Greece: "For the Athenians command the rest of Greece, I command the

Athenians, your mother commands me, and you command your mother."

Lives. Themistocles. Page 145

Be ruled by time, the wisest counsellor of all.

Lives. Pericles. Page 198

Old women should not seek to be perfumed.

Lives. Pericles. Page 203

Trees, when they are lopped and cut, grow up again in a short time, but men, being once lost, cannot easily be recovered.

Lives. Pericles. Page 207

He said that in his whole life he most repented of three things: one was that he had trusted a secret to a woman; another, that he went by water when he might have gone by land; the third, that he had remained one whole day without doing any business of moment.

Lives. Marcus Cato. Page 418

Where the lion's skin will not reach, you must patch it out with the fox's.

Lives. Lysander. Page 529

The whole life of man is but a point of time; let us enjoy it, therefore, while it lasts, and not spend it to no purpose.

Of the Training of Children.

Like the man who threw a stone at a bitch, but hit his step-mother, on which he exclaimed, "Not so bad!"

On the Tranquillity of the Mind

When the candles are out all women are fair.

Conjugal Precepts

PLINY THE YOUNGER
(A.D. 61-105)

That indolent but agreeable condition of doing nothing.

Letters. Book VIII, Letter 9,3

His only fault is that he has no fault.

Letters. Book IX, Letter 26, 1

MARCUS AURELIUS ANTONINUS
(A.D. 121-180)

As for life, it is a battle and a sojourning in a strange land; but the fame that comes after is oblivion.

Meditations. II,17

Waste not the remnant of thy life in those imaginations touching other folk, whereby thou contributest not to the common weal.

Meditations. III,4

A man should *be* upright, not be *kept* upright.

Meditations. III, 5

Nothing can come out of nothing, any more than a thing can go back to nothing.

Meditations. IV, 4

Death like birth, is a secret of Nature.

Meditations. IV. 5

"Let thine occupations be few," saith the sage, "if thou wouldst lead a tranquil life."

Meditations. IV, 24

Remember this,—that there is a proper dignity and proportion to be observed in the performance of every act of life.

Meditations. IV, 32

Time is a sort of river of passing events, and strong is its current; no sooner is a thing brought to sight than it is swept by and another takes its place, and this too will be swept away.

Meditations. IV, 43

Remember that to change thy mind and to follow him that sets thee right, is to be the less the free agent that thou wast before.

Meditations. VIII, 16

DIOGENES LAERTIUS
(Circa A.D. 200)

Solon gave the following advice: "Consider your honour, as a gentleman, of more weight than an oath."

Solon. 12

Epimenides was sent by his father into the field to look for a sheep, turned out of the road at mid-day and lay down in a certain cave and fell asleep, and slept there fifty-seven years; and after that, when awake, he went on looking for the sheep, thinking that he had been taking a short nap.

Epimenides. 2

He said that there was one only good, namely, knowledge; and one only evil, namely ignorance.

Socrates. 14

Being asked whether it was better to marry or not, he replied, "Whichever you do, you will repent it."

Socrates. 16

The question was put to him, what hope is; and his answer was, "That dream of a waking man."

Aristotle. II

The question was once put to him, how we ought to behave to our friends; and the answer he gave was, "As we should wish our friends to behave to us."

Aristotle. II

Plato having defined man to be a two-legged animal without feathers, Diogenes plucked a cock and brought it into the Academy, and said, "This is Plato's man." On which account this addition was made to the definition,—"With broad flat nails."

Diogenes. 6

A man once asked Diogenes what was the proper time for supper, and he made answer, "If you are a rich man, whenever you please; and if you are a poor man, whenever you can."

Diogenes. 6

Diogenes lighted a candle in the daytime, and went round saying, "I am looking for a man."

Diogenes. 6

When asked what he would take to let a man give him a blow on the head, he said, "A helmet."

Diogenes. 6

Once he saw a youth blushing, and addressed him, "Courage,

my boy! that is the complexion of virtue."

Diogenes. 6

When asked what wine he liked to drink, he replied, "That which belongs to another."

Diogenes. 6

When a man reproached him for going into unclean places, he said, "The sun too penetrates into privies, but is not polluted by them."

Diogenes. 6

When Zeno was asked what a friend was, he replied, "Another I."

Zeno. 19

They say that the first inclination which an animal has is to protect itself.

Zeno. 52

Epicurus laid down the doctrine that pleasure was the chief good.

Epicurus. 6

MOSES BEN MAIMON (MAIMONIDES) (1135-1204)

Anticipate charity by preventing poverty; assist the reduced fellowman, either by a considerable gift, or a sum of money, or by teaching him a trade, or by putting him in the way of business, so that he may earn an honest livelihood, and not be forced to the dreadful alternative of holding out his hand for charity. This is the highest step and the summit of charity's golden ladder.

Charity's Eight Degrees

ST. THOMAS AQUINAS (Circa 1225-1274)

Three things are necessary for the salvation of man: to know what he ought to believe; to know what he ought to desire; and to know what he ought to do.

Two Precepts of Charity (1273)

DANTE ALIGHIERI
(1265-1321)

In the middle of the journey of our life I came to myself in a dark wood where the straight way was lost.

Divine Comedy (Circa 1300)
Inferno, Canto I, Line I

Consider your origin; ye were not formed to live like brutes, but to follow virtue and knowledge.

Divine Comedy, Inferno
Canto XXVI, Line 119

O human race, born to fly upward, wherefore at a little wind dost thou so fall.

Divine Comedy, Purgatorio
Canto XII, Line 95

Great flame follows a tiny spark.

Divine Comedy, Paradiso
Canto I, Line 34

The greatest gift which God in His bounty bestowed in creating, and the most conformed to His own goodness, and that which He prizes the most, was the freedom of the will, with which the creatures that have intelligence, they all and they alone, were and are endowed.

Divine Comedy, Paradiso
Canto V, Line 19

GEOFFREY CHAUCER (?1343-1400)

Hard is the herte that loveth nought in May.

The Romaunt of the Rose
(Circa 1369). Line 85

Morpheus,
Thous knowest hym wel, the god of slep.

The Book of the Duchesse
(1369) Line 136

Trewe as stiel.

Troilus and Criseyde. Book V,
Line 831

Nowher so bisy a man as he ther nas,
And yet he semed bisier than he was.
The Canterbury Tales. Prologue,
Line 321

Love is blynd.
The Canterbury Tales
The Merchant's Tale, Line 1598

FRANCOIS RABELAIS
(1495-1553)

Let down the curtain: the farce is done.
Life of Rabelais

By robbing Peter he paid Paul, . . . and hoped to catch larks if ever the heavens should fall.
Works. Book I, Chap. 11

How shall I be able to rule over others, that have not full power and command of myself?
Book I, Chap. 52

Subject to a kind of disease, which at that time they called lack of money.
Book II (1534), Chap. 16

He did not care a button for it.
Book II (1534), Chap. 16

How well I feathered my nest.
Ibid. Book II (1534) Chap. 17

Plain as a nose in a man's face.
Book V, Author's Prologue

And thereby hangs a tale.
Book V, Chap. 4

What cannot be cured must be endured.
Book V, Chap. 15

JOHN HEYWOOD
(1497-1580)

Two heads are better then one.
Proverbes. Part I, Chap. IX

To tell tales out of schoole.
Proverbes. Part I, Chap. X

All is well that ends well.
Proverbes. Part I, Chap. X

Beggars should be no choosers.
Proverbes. Part I, Chap. X

A man may well bring a horse to the water
But he cannot make him drinke without he will.
Proverbes. Part I, Chap. X

Better is halfe a lofe than no bread.
Proverbes. Part I, Chap. XI

A peny for your thought.
Proverbes. Part II, Chap. IV

There is no fire without some smoke.
Proverbes. Part II, Chap. V

MICHEL DE MONTAIGNE
(1533-1592)

The thing of which I have most fear is fear.
Essays. Book I, Chap. 17
Of Fear

There are some defeats more triumphant than victories.
Essays. Book I, Chap. 30
Of Cannibals

Let us a little permit Nature to taker her own way; she better understands her own affairs than we.
Essays. Book III, Chap. 13
Of Experience

MIGUEL DE CERVANTES
(1547-1616)

You are a King by your own Fireside, as much as any Monarch in his Throne.
Don Quixote (1605-1615)
The Author's Preface

Can we ever have too much of a good thing?

Don Quixote (1605-1615)
Part I, Book I, Chap. 6

Fortune leaves always some door open to come at a remedy.

Don Quixote, Part I, Book III, Chap. 1

To give the devil his due.

Don Quixote, Part I, Book III, Chap. 3

A peck of troubles.

Don Quixote, Part I, Book III, Chap. 4

You're leaping over the hedge before you come to the stile.

Don Quixote, Part I, Book III
Chap. 4

Paid him in his own coin.

Don Quixote, Part I, Book III, Chap. 4

Bell, book, and candle.

Don Quixote, Part I, Book III, Chap. 4

Every tooth in a man's head is more valuable than a diamond.

Don Quixote, Part I, Book III, Chap. 4

A finger in every pie.

Don Quixote, Part I, Book III, Chap. 6

Every dog has his day.

Don Quixote, Part I, Book III, Chap. 6

You may go whistle for the rest.

Don Quixote, Part I, Book III, Chap. 6

Why do you lead me a wild-goose chase?

Don Quixote, Part I, Book III, Chap. 6

Those who'll play with cats must expect to be scratched.

Don Quixote, Part I, Book III, Chap. 8

Raise a hue and cry.

Don Quixote, Part I, Book III, Chap. 8

Absence, that common cure of love.

Don Quixote, Part I, Book III, Chap. 10

As much a fool as he was, he loved money, and knew how to keep it when he had it, and was wise enough to keep his own counsel.

Don Quixote, Part I, Book III, Chap. 13

My honour is dearer to me than my life.
Don Quixote, Part I, Book IV, Chap. 1

I begin to smell a rat.
Don Quixote, Part I, Book IV, Chap. 10

I'll take my corporal oath on 't.
Don Quixote, Part I, Book IV, Chap. 10

The proof of the pudding is in the eating.
Don Quixote, Part I, Book IV, Chap. 10

Let none presume to tell me that the pen is preferable to the sword.
Don Quixote, Part I, Book IV, Chap. 10

Birds of a feather flock together.
Don Quixote, Part II, Book III, Chap. 4

Fore-warned, fore-armed.
Don Quixote, Part II, Book III, Chap. 10

I'll turn over a new leaf.
Don Quixote, Part III, Book III, Chap. 13

Honesty's the best policy.
Don Quixote, Part II, Book III, Chap. 33

An honest man's word is as good as his bond.
Don Quixote, Part II, Book IV, Chap. 34

The pot calls the kettle black.
Don Quixote, Part II, Book IV, Chap. 38

When thou art at Rome, do as they do at Rome.
Don Quixote, Part II, Book IV, Chap. 54

SIR WALTER RALEIGH
(1552-1618)

If all the world and love were young,
And truth in every shepherd's tongue,
These pretty pleasures might me move
To live with thee, and be thy love.
The Nymph's Reply to the Passionate
Shepherd Printed in England's
Helicon (1600) Stanza I

EDMUND SPENSER
(?1553-1599)

Roses red and violets blew,
And all the sweetest flowres, that in the forrest grew.

The Faerie Queens, Book III
Canto 6, Stanza 6

For deeds doe die, how ever noblie donne,
And thoughts of men do as themselves decay,
but wise wordes taught in numbers for to runne,
Recorded by the Muses, live for ay.

The Ruines of Time (1591). Line 400

Though last not least.

Colin Clouts Come Home Again
(1595). Line 144

GEORGE CHAPMAN
(1559-1634)

Promise is most given when the least is said.

Hero and Leander (1598)

Young men think old men are fools; but old men know young men are fools.

All Fools (1605), Act V, Sc. I

Who to himself is law no law doth need,
Offends no law, and is a king indeed.

Bussy D'Ambois (1607), Act II, Sc. I

Give me a spirit that on this life's rough sea
Loves t'have his sails fill'd with a lust wind,
Even till his sail-yards tremble, his masts crack,
And his rapt ship run on her side so low
That she drinks water, and her keel plows air.

Conspiracy of Charles, Duke of
Byron (1608), Act III, Sc. I

SIR JOHN HARINGTON
(1561-1612)

The readers and the hearers like my books,

But yet some writers cannot them digest;
But what care I? for when I make a feast
I would my guests should praise it, not the cooks.

Epigrams. Of Writers Who Carp
at Other Men's Books

FRANCIS BACON
(1561-1626)

The monuments of wit survive the monuments of power.

Essex's Device (1595)

I do plainly and ingeniously confess that I am guilty of corruption, and do renounce all defense. I beseech your Lordships to be merciful to a broken reed.

On being charged by Parliament
with corruption in the exercise
of his office (1621).

Like the strawberry wives, that laid two or three great strawberries at the mouth of their pot, and all the rest were little ones.

Apothegms (1624) No. 54

No pleasure is comparable to the standing upon the vantage-ground of truth.

Of Truth

Men fear death as children fear to go in the dark; and as that natural fear in children is increased with tales, so is the other.

Of Death

A good name is like a precious ointment; it filleth all around about, and will not easily away; for the odors of ointments are more durable than those of flowers.

Of Praise

Mahomet made the people believe that he would call a hill to him, and from the top of it offer up his prayers for the observers of his law. The people assembled. Mahomet called the hill to come to him, again and again; and when the hill stood still he was never a whit abashed, but said, "If the hill will not come to Mahomet, Mahomet will go to the hill."

Of Boldness

In things that a man would not be seen in himself, it is a point of cunning to borrow the name of the world; as to say, "The world says," or "There is a speech abroad."

Of Cunning

There is a cunning which we in England call "the turning of the cat in the pan," which is, when that which a man says to another, he lays it as if another had said it to him.

Of Cunning

Some books are to be tasted, others to be swallowed, and some few to be chewed and digested.

Of Studies

Reading maketh a full man, conference a ready man, and writing an exact man.

Of Studies

Histories make men wise; poets, witty; the mathematics, subtile; natural philosophy, deep; moral, grave; logic and rhetoric, able to contend.

Of Studies

CHRISTOPHER MARLOWE
(1564-1593)

I'm armed with more than complete steel,—
The justice of my quarrel.

Lust's Dominion. Act III, Sc. 4

By shallow rivers, to whose falls
Melodious birds sing madrigals.

The Passionate Shepherd to his Love (1599)

And I will make thee beds of roses
And a thousand fragrant posies.

The Passionate Shepherd to his Love (1599)

Hell hath no limits, nor is circumscribed
In one self-place; for what we are is Hell,
And where Hell is, there must we ever be.

Doctor Faustus. (1604) Sc. 5

Was this the face that launch'd a thousand ships
And burnt the topless towers of Ilium?
Sweet Helen, make me immortal with a kiss!
Her lips suck forth my soul: see, where it flies.

Doctor Faustus. Sc. 14

I count religion but a childish toy,
And hold there is no sin but ignorance.

*The Jew of Malta (Published
1633). Act I*

WILLIAM SHAKESPEARE
(1564-1616)

Glory is like a circle in the water,
Which never ceaseth to enlarge itself,
Till by broad spreading it disperse to nought.

*King Henry VI, (1591) Part I,
Act I, Sc. 2, Line 133*

She's beautiful and therefore to be wooed,
She is a woman, therefore to be won.

*King Henry VI, Part I, Act V,
Sc. 3, Line 78*

Could I come near your beauty with my nails
I'd set my ten commandments in your face.

*King Henry VI, Part II, Act I,
Sc. 3, Line 144*

And many strokes, though with a little axe,
Hew down and fell the hardest-timbered oak.

*King Henry VI, Part III,
Act II, Sc. I, Line 54*

To weep is to make less the depth of grief.

*King Henry VI, Part III,
Act II, Sc. I, Line 85*

Thus far into the bowels of the land
Have we marched on without impediment.

*King Richard III, Act V,
Sc. 2, Line 3*

A horse! a horse! my kingdom for a horse!

King Richard III, Act V,
Sc. 4, Line 7

And if the boy have not a woman's gift
To rain a shower of commanded tears,
An onion will do well for such a shift.

The Taming of the Shrew (1593-1594)
Induction, Sc. I, Line 124

No profit grows where is no pleasure ta'en;
In brief, sir, study what you most affect.

The Taming of the Shrew (1593-1594)
Act I, Sc. I, Line 39

There's small choice in rotten apples.

The Taming of the Shrew (1593-1594)
Act I, Sc. I, Line 137

There's small choice in rotten apples.

The Taming of the Shrew (1593-1594)
Act I, Sc. I, Line 137

Such duty as the subject owes the prince,
Even such a woman oweth to her husband.

The Taming of the Shrew.
Act V, Sc. 2, Line 156

Love is a spirit all compact of fire.

Venus and Adonis (1593) Line 149

Time's glory is to calm contending kings,
To unmask falsehood, and bring truth to light.

The Rape of Lucrece. Line 939

They do not love that do not show their love.

The Two Gentlemen of Verona
(1594-1595). Act I, Sc. 1, Line 31

He makes sweet music.

The Two Gentlemen of Verona
Act II, Sc. 7, Line 28

That man that hath a tongue, I say, is no man.
If with his tongue he cannot win a woman.

The Two Gentlemen of Verona
Act III, Sc. I, Line 104

It seems she hangs upon the cheek of night
Like a rich jewel in an Ethiop's ear;
Beauty too rich for use, for earth too dear.

Romeo and Juliet, Act I, Sc. 5
Line 49

O Romeo, Romeo! wherefore art thou Romeo?
Deny thy father, and refuse thy name;
Or, if thou wilt not, be but sworn my love,
And I'll no longer be a Capulet.

Romeo and Juliet, Act II
Sc. 2, Line 33

What's in a name? That which we call a rose
By any other name would smell as sweet.

Romeo and Juliet, Act II
Sc. 2, Line 43

Good night, good night! parting is such sweet sorrow,
That I shall say good night till it be morrow.

Romeo and Juliet, Act II
Sc. 2, Line 184

And nothing can we call our own but death;
And that small model of the barren earth,
Which serves as paste and cover to our bones.
For God's sake, let us sit upon the ground,
And tell sad stories of the death of kings:
How some have been deposed, some slain in war,
Some haunted by the ghosts they have depos'd
Some poison'd by their wives, some sleeping kill'd;
All murder'd: for within the hollow crown
That rounds the mortal temples of a king
Keeps Death his court.

King Richard II, Act III
Sc. 2, Line 152

The eye of man hath not heard, the ear of man hath not seen,
man's hand is not able to taste, his tongue to conceive, nor his
heart to report, what my dream was.

A Midsummer-Night's Dream
Act IV, Sc. I, Line 218

With the help of a surgeon, he might yet recover and prove an ass.

A Midsummer-Night's Dream
Act V, Sc. I, Line 318

Tne iron tongue of midnight hath told twelve.

A Midsummer-Night's Dream
Act V, Sc. I, Line 372

I am a Jew. Hath not a Jew eyes? Hath not a Jew hands, organs, dimensions, senses, affections, passions?

The Merchant of Venice
Act III, Sc. I, Line 62

If you prick us, do we not bleed? If you tickle us, do we not laugh? if you poison us, do we not die? and if you wrong us, shall we not revenge?

The Merchant of Venice
Act III, Sc. I, Line 65

The weakest kind of fruit
Drops earliest to the ground.

The Merchant of Venice
Act IV, Sc. I, Line 115

The quality of mercy is not strain'd,
It droppeth as the gentle rain from heaven
Upon the place beneath. It is twice bless'd:
It blesseth him that gives and him that takes.

The Merchant of Venice
Act IV, Sc. I, Line 184

Life is as tedious as a twice-told tale,
Vexing the dull ear of a drowsy man.

King John, Act III, Sc. 4, Line 108

When Fortune means to men most good,
She looks upon them with a threatening eye.

King John, Act III, Sc. 4, Line 119

To gild refined gold, to paint the lily,
To throw a perfume on the violet,
To smooth the ice, or add another hue
Unto the rainbow, or with taper-light
To seek the beauteous eye of heaven to garnish,

Is wasteful and ridiculous excess.

King John, Act IV, Sc. 2, Line II

From the crown of his head to the sole of his foot, he is all mirth.

Much Ado About Nothing
Act III, Sc. 2, Line 9

He hath a heart as sound as a bell, and his tongue is the clapper; for what his heart thinks his tongue speaks.

Much Ado About Nothing
Act III, Sc. 2, Line 12

Sweet are the uses of adversity;
Which, like the toad, ugly and venomous,
Wears yet a precious jewel in his head;
And this our life, exempt from public haunt,
Finds tongues in trees, books in the running brooks,
Sermons in stones, and good in every thing.

As You Like It
Act II, Sc. 1, Line 12

Under the greenwood tree
Who loves to lie with me,
And turn his merry note
Unto the sweet bird's throat,
Come hither, come hither, come hither:
  Here shall he see
  No enemy
But winter and rough weather.

As You Like It
Act II, Sc. 5, Line 1

And so from hour to hour we ripe and ripe,
And then from hour to hour we rot and rot;
And thereby hangs a tale.

As You Like It
Act II, Sc. 7, Line 26

All the world's a stage,
And all the men and women merely players.
They have their exits and their entrances;
And one man in his time plays many parts,

His acts being seven ages. At first the infant,
Mewling and puking in the nurse's arms.
And then the whining school-boy, with his satchel
And shining morning face, creeping like snail
Unwillingly to school. And then the lover,
Sighing like furnace, with a woeful ballad
Made to his mistress' eyebrow. Then a soldier
Full of strange oaths, and bearded like the pard;
Jealous in honour, sudden and quick in quarrel,
Seeking the bubble reputation
Even in the cannon's mouth. And then the justice,
In fair round belly with good capon lined,
With eyes severe and beard of formal cut,
Full of wise saws and modern instances;
And so he plays his part. The sixth age shifts
Into the lean and slipper'd pantaloon,
With spectacles on nose and pouch on side;
His youthful hose, well saved, a world too wide
For his shrunk shank; and his big manly voice,
Turning again toward childish treble, pipes
And whistles in his sound. Last scene of all,
That ends this strange eventful history,
Is second childishness, and mere oblivion,
Sans teeth, sans eyes, sans taste, sans everything.

As You Like It
Act II, Sc. 7, Line 139

It was a lover and his lass,
With a hey, and a ho, and hey nonino,
That o'er the green cornfield did pass,
In the spring time, the only pretty ring time,
When birds do sing, hey ding a ding, ding;
Sweet lovers love the spring.

As You Like It
Act V, Sc. 3, Line 18

Rich honesty dwells like a miser, sir, in a poor house; as your pearl in your foul oyster.

As You Like It
Act V, Sc. 4, Line 62

The fault, dear Brutus, is not in our stars,
But in ourselves, that we are underlings.

Julius Caesar, Act I, Sc. 2, Line 134

Cowards die many times before their deaths;
The valiant never taste of death but once.

Julius Caesar, Act II, Sc. 2, Line 32

How hard it is for women to keep counsel.

Julius Caesar,
Act II, Sc. 4, Line 9

Romans, countrymen, and lovers! hear me for my cause; and
be silent, that you may hear.

Julius Caesar, Act III
Sc. 2, Line 13

Not that I loved Caesar less, but that I loved Rome more.

Julius Caesar, Act III
Sc. 2, Line 22

As he was valiant I honour him: but, as he was ambitious, I slew
him.

Julius Caesar, Act III
Sc. 2, Line 27

Friends, Romans, countrymen, lend me your ears;
I come to bury Caesar, not to praise him.
The evil that men do lives after them,
The good is oft interred with their bones.

Julius Caesar, Act III
Sc. 2, Line 79

For Brutus is an honourable man;
So are they all, all honourable men.

Julius Caesar, Act III
Sc. 2, Line 88

When that the poor have cried, Caesar hath wept;
Ambition should be made of sterner stuff.

Julius Caesar, Act III
Sc. 2, Line 97

There are more things in heaven and earth, Horatio,
Than are dreamt of in your philosophy.

Hamlet, Act I, Sc. 5, Line 166

To be, or not to be: that is the question:
Whether 'tis nobler in the mind to suffer
The slings and arrows of outrageous fortune,
Or to take arms against a sea of troubles,
And by opposing end them? To die: to sleep:

Hamlet, Act III, Sc. 1, Line 56

The lady doth protest too much, methinks.

Hamlet, Act III, Sc. 2, Line 242

We know what we are, but know not what we may be.

Hamlet, Act IV, Sc. 5, Line 72

When sorrows come, they come not single spies,
But in battalions.

Hamlet, Act IV, Sc. 5, Line 78

Our bodies are our gardens, to the which our wills are
gardeners; ...
either to have it sterile with idleness or manured with
industry.

Othello, Act I, Sc. 3, Line 324

I'll example you with thievery:
The sun's a thief, and with his great attraction
Robs the vast sea; the moon's an arrant thief,
And her pale fire she snatches from the sun;
The sea's a thief, whose liquid surge resolves
The moon into salt tears; the earth's a thief,
That feeds and breeds by a composture stolen
From general excrement; each thing's a thief.

Timon of Athens, Act IV
Sc. 2, Line 441

Had I but served my God with half the zeal
I served my king, he would not in mine age
Have left me naked to mine enemies.

King Henry VIII, Act III
Sc. 2, Line 456

He was a man
Of an unbounded stomach.

King Henry VIII, Act IV
Sc. 2, Line 33

BEN JONSON
(1573?-1637)

True happiness
Consists not in the multitude of friends,
But in the worth and choice.

Cynthia's Revels (1600)
Act III, Sc. 2

The dignity of truth is lost with much protesting.

Catiline's Conspiracy (1611)
Act III, Sc. 2

GEORGE HERBERT
(1593-1633)

Dare to be true: nothing can need a lie;
A fault which needs it most, grows two thereby.

The Temple, The Church Porch
Stanza 13

By all means use sometimes to be alone.

The Temple, The Church Porch
Stanza 25

Love, and a cough, cannot be hid.

Jacula Prudentum (1640)

Deceive not thy physician, confessor, nor lawyer.

Jacula Prudentum

Whose house is of glass, must not throw stones at another.

Jacula Prudentum

Time is the rider that breaks youth.

Jacula Prudentum

Show me a liar, and I will show thee a thief.

Jacula Prudentum

One father is more than a hundred school-masters.

Jacula Prudentum

IZAAK WALTON
(1593-1683)

I have laid aside business, and gone a-fishing.
The Compleat Angler (1653-1655)
Author's Preface

Angling may be said to be so like the mathematics that it can never be fully learnt.
The Compleat Angler,
Author's Preface

As the Italians say, Good company in a journey makes the way to seem the shorter.
The Compleat Angler, Part I, Chap. I

You will find angling to be like the virtue of humility, which has a calmness of spirit and a world of other blessings attending upon it.
The Compleat Angler, Part I, Chap. I

RENE DESCARTES
(1596-1650)

I think, therefore I am.
Le Discours de la Methode (1637)

Good sense is of all things in the world the most equally distributed, for everybody thinks himself so abundantly provided with it, that even those most difficult to please in all other matters do not commonly desire more of it than they already possess.
Le Discours de la Methode (1637)

The greatest minds are capable of the greatest vices as well as of the greatest virtues.
Le Discours de la Methode (1637)

OLIVER CROMWELL
(1599-1658)

I would have been glad to have lived under my woodside, and

to have kept a flock of sheep, rather than to have undertaken this government.

To Parliament (1658)

I would be willing to live to be further serviceable to God and His people but my work is done! Yet God will be with His people!

(September 1, 1658, two days before his death)

SAMUEL BUTLER
(1600-1680)

When civil fury first grew high,
And men fell out they knew not why.

Hudibras, Part I (1663),
Canto I, Line 1

SIR THOMAS BROWNE
(1605-1682)

A man may be in as just possession of truth as of a city, and yet be forced to surrender.

Religio Medici (1642)
Part I, Sec. VI

But how shall we expect charity towards others, when we are uncharitable to our selves? *Charity begins at home,* is the voice of the world; yet is every man his greatest enemy, and, as it were, his own executioner.

Religio Medici, Part II, Sec. IV

For the world, I count it not an inn, but an hospital; and a place not to live, but to die in.

Religio Medici, Part II, Sec. IX

JOHN MILTON
(1608-1674)

How soon hath Time, the subtle thief of youth,
Stol'n on his wing my three-and-twentieth year.

On His Having Arrived at the Age of Twenty-three (1631)

Mirth, admit me of thy crew,

To live with her, and live with thee,
In unreproved pleasures free.

L'Allegro (1632), Line 38

Love Virtue, she alone is free,
She can teach ye how to climb
Higher than the sphery chime;
Or, if Virtue feeble were,
Heav'n itself would stoop to her.

Comus, Line 1019

What in me is dark
Illumine, what is low raise and support;
That to the height of this great argument
I may assert eternal Providence,
And justify the ways of God to men.

Paradise Lost (1667), Book I, Line 22

Where peace
And rest can never dwell, hope never comes
That comes to all.

Paradise Lost (1667), Book I, Line 65

What honour that,
But tedious waste of time, to sit and hear
So many hollow compliments and lies,
Outlandish flatteries?

Paradise Regained, Book IV, Line 122

The childhood shows the man,
As morning shows the day.

Paradise Regained, Book IV, Line 220

The sun to me is dark
And silent as the moon,
When she deserts the night,
Hid in her vacant interlunar cave.

Samson Agonistes, Line 86

SIR JOHN SUCKLING
(1609-1642)

Death's no punishment: it is the sense,

The pains and fears afore, that makes a death.
Aglaura (1638), Act V, Sc. 1

Her feet beneath her petticoat
Like little mice, stole in and out,
As if they feared the light;
But oh, she dances such a way!
No sun upon an Easter-day
Is half so fine a sight.
A Ballad upon a Wedding (1641)
Stanza 8

Women are the baggage of life: they are
Troublesome, and hinder us in the great march,
And yet we cannot be without 'em.
The Tragedy of Brennoralt (1646)
Act I, Sc. I

Success is a rare paint, hides all the ugliness.
The Tragedy of Brennoralt (1646)
Act I, Sc. I

JEREMY TAYLOR
(1613-1667)

Every man hath in his own life sins enough, in his own mind trouble enough: so that curiosity after the affairs of others cannot be without envy and an evil mind. What is it to me if my neighbour's grandfather were a Syrian, or his grandmother illegitimate, or that another is indebted five thousand pounds, or whether his wife be expensive?
Holy Living (1650-1651)

FRANCOIS, DUC DE LA
ROCHEFOUCAULD
(1613-1680)

Self-interest speaks all sorts of tongues, and plays all sorts of roles, even that of disinterestedness.
Maxim 39

We are never so happy nor so unhappy as we imagine.
Maxim 49

To succeed in the world, we do everything we can to appear successful.

Maxim 56

There is no disguise which can for long conceal love where it exists or simulate it where it does not.

Maxim 70

There are very few people who are not ashamed of having been in love when they no longer love each other.

Maxim 71

True love is like ghosts, which everybody talks about and few have seen.

Maxim 76

The love of justice is simply, in the majority of men, the fear of suffering injustice.

Maxim 78

Silence is the best tactic for him who distrusts himself.

Maxim 79

RICHARD LOVELACE
(1618-1658)

Oh, could you view the melody
Of every grace
And music of her face,
You'd drop a tear;
Seeing more harmony
In her bright eye
Than now you hear.

Orpheus to Beasts (1649)

JEAN BAPTISTE MOLIERE
(1622-1673)

The world, dear Agnes, is a strange affair.

L'Ecole des Femmes (1662), Act II, Sc. 6

He's a wonderful talker, who has the art of telling you nothing in a great harangue.

Le Misanthrope (1666), Act II, Sc. 5

If everyone were clothed with integrity, if every heart were just, frank, kindly, the other virtues would be well-nigh useless, since their chief purpose is to make us bear with patience the injustice of our fellows.

Le Misanthrope (1666), Act V, Sc. 1

One must eat to live, and not live to eat.

Amphitryon (1668), Act III, Sc. 1

BLAISE PASCAL
(1623-1662)

Things are always at their best in their beginning.

Lettres Provinciales (1656-1657)
No. 4

Too much and too little education hinder the mind.

Pensees (1670), Sect. II, No. 72

I lay it down as a fact that, if all men knew what others say of them, there would not be four friends in the world.

Pensees (1670), Sect. II, No. 101

JOHN BUNYAN
(1628-1688)

And so I penned
It down, until at last it came to be,
For length and breadth, the bigness which you see.

Pilgrim's Progress (1678)
Apology for His Book

The pilgrim they laid in a large upper chamber, whose window opened toward the sun-rising; the name of the chamber was Peace.

Pilgrim's Progress (1678)
Apology for His Book, Part I

It beareth the name of Vanity Fair, because the town where 'tis kept is lighter than vanity.

Pilgrim's Progress, Part I

JOHN DRYDEN
(1631-1700)

I am resolved to grow fat, and look young till forty.
Secret Love, or the Maiden Queen
(1667), Act III, Sc. 1

Bankrupt of life, yet prodigal of ease.
Absalom and Achitophel
Part I (1680), Line 168

And all to leave what with his toil he won
To that unfeather'd two-legg'd thing, a son.
Absalom and Achitophel
Part I (1680), Line 169

His tribe were God Almighty's gentlemen.
Absalom and Achitophel
Part I, Line 645

Large was his wealth, but larger was his heart.
Absalom and Achitophel
Part I, Line 826

Happy the man, and happy he alone,
He who can call today his own;
He who, secure within, can say,
Tomorrow, do thy worst, for I have liv'd today.
Imitation of Horace, Book III
Ode 29 (1685), Line 65

BENEDICT (BARUCH) SPINOZA
(1632-1677)

Nature abhors a vacuum.
Ethics (1677) Part I,
Prop. XV, Note

God and all the attributed of God are eternal.
Ethics (1677) Part I
Prop. XIX

Nothing exists from whose nature some effect does not follow.
Ethics (1677) Part I
Prop. XXXVI

He who would distinguish the true from the false must have an adequate idea of what is true and false.

Ethics (1677) Part II
Prop. XLII, Proof

Will and Intellect are one and the same thing.

Ethics (1677) Part II
Prop. XLIX, Corollary

Fear cannot be without hope nor hope without fear.

Ethics (1677) Definition XIII
Explanation

One and the same thing can at the same time be good, bad, and indifferent, e.g., music is good to the melancholy, bad to those who mourn, and neither good nor bad to the deaf.

Ethics, Part IV, Preface

Man is a social animal.

Ethics, Prop. XXXV, Note

Fame has also this great drawback, that if we pursue it we must direct our lives in such a way as to please the fancy of men, avoiding what they dislike and seeking what is pleasing to them.

Tractatus de Intellectus
Emendatione (1677) 1, 5

The more intelligible a thing is, the more easily it is retained in the memory, and contrariwise, the less intelligible it is, the more easily we forget it.

Tractatus de Intellectus
Emendatione (1677) XI, 81

JOHN LOCKE
(1632-1704)

New opinions are always suspected, and usually opposed, without any other reason but because they are not already common.

Essay on Human Understanding
(1690) Dedicatory Epistle

It is one thing to show a man that he is in error, and another to put him in possession of truth.

Essay on Human Understanding
(1690) Book IV, Chap. 7, Sect. II

All men are liable to error; and most men are, in many points, by passion or interest, under temptation to it.

Essay on Human Understanding
(1690) Book IV, Chap. 20, Sect. 17

He that will have his son have a respect for him and his orders, must himself have a great reverence for his son.

Some Thoughts on Education (1693)
Section 65

The only fence against the world is a thorough knowledge of it.

Some Thoughts on Education (1693)
Section 88

SAMUEL PEPYS
(1633-1703)

I pray God to keep me from being proud.

Diary, March 22, 1660

This day I am, by the blessing of God, 34 years old, in very good health and mind's content, and in condition of estate much beyond whatever my friends could expect of a child of their's, this day 34 years. The Lord's name be praised! and may I be thankful for it.

Diary, February 23, 1667

SIR ISAAC NEWTON
(1642-1727)

I do not know what I may appear to the world; but to myself I seem to have been only like a boy playing on the seashore, and diverting myself in now and then finding a smoother pebble or a prettier shell than ordinary, whilst the great ocean of truth lay all undiscovered before me.

Brewster's Memoirs of Newton
(1855) Vol. II, Chap. XXVII

WILLIAM PENN
(1644-1718)

The receipts of cookery are swelled to a volume; but a good stomach excels them all.

Fruits of Solitude (1693)

Truth often suffers more by the heat of its defenders, than from the arguments of its opposers.

Fruits of Solitude (1693)

Men are generally more careful of the breed of their horses and dogs than of their children.

Fruits of Solitude (1693)

DANIEL DEFOE
(1661-1731)

Wherever God erects a house of prayer,
The Devil always builds a chapel there;
And 'twill be found, upon examination,
The latter has the largest congregation.

*The True-Born Englishman
(1701) Part I, Line I*

I let him know his name should be Friday, which was the day I saved his life.

Robinson Crusoe (1719)

I took my man Friday with me.

Robinson Crusoe (1719)

MATTHEW PRIOR
(1664-1721)

Be to her virtues very kind;
Be to her faults a little blind.
Let all her ways be unconfin'd:
And clap your padlock—on her mind!

An English Padlock (1707)

JONATHAN SWIFT
(1667-1745)

Satire is a sort of glass, wherein beholders do generally discover everybody's face but their own.

Battle of the Books (1704)
Preface

The two noblest things, which are sweetness and light.

Battle of the Books (1704)
Preface

Conversation is but carving!
Give no more to every guest
Than he's able to digest.
Give him always of the prime,
And but little at a time.
Carve to all but just enough,
Let them neither starve nor stuff,
And that you may have your due,
Let your neighbor carve for you.

Conversation

May you live all the days of your life.

Polite Conversation. Dialogue II

I always like to begin a journey on Sundays, because I shall have the prayers of the Church to preserve all that travel by land or by water.

Polite Conversation. Dialogue II

I know Sir John will go, though he was sure it would rain cats and dogs.

Polite Conversation. Dialogue II

Hail, fellow, well met,
All dirty and wet:
Find out if you can,
Who's master, who's man.

My Lady's Lamentation (1765)
Line 171

WILLIAM CONGREVE
(1670-1729)

Eternity was in that moment.

> *The Old Bachelor (1693) Act IV, Sc. 7*

It is the business of a comic poet to paint the vices and follies of human kind.

> *The Double Dealer (1694)*
> *Epistle Dedicatory*

Music hath charms to soothe the savage breast,
To soften rocks, or bend a knotted oak.

> *The Mourning Bride (1607)*
> *Act I, Sc. 1*

Heaven has no rage like love to hatred turned,
Nor hell a fury like a woman scorned.

> *The Mourning Bride (1607)*
> *Act III, Sc. 8*

Defer not till tomorrow to be wise,
Tomorrow's sun to thee may never rise.

> *Letter to Cobham*

JOSEPH ADDISON
(1672-1719)

Reading is to the mind what exercise is to the body.

> *The Tatler (1709-1711), No. 147*

Soon as the evening shades prevail,
The moon takes up the wondrous tale,
And nightly to the listening earth
Repeats the story of her birth;
While all the stars that round her burn,
And all the planets in their turn,
Confirm the tidings as they roll,
And spread the truth from pole to pole.

> *Ode (in The Spectator, No. 465,*
> *August 23, 1712)*

True happiness is of a retired nature, and an enemy to pomp and noise; it arises, in the first place, from the enjoyment of one's self; and, in the next, from the friendship and conversation of a few select companions.

The Spectator, No. 15, March 17, 1711

Books are the legacies that a great genius leaves to mankind, which are delivered down from generation to generation, as presents to the posterity of those who are yet unborn.

The Spectator, No. 166
September 10, 1711

A true critic ought to dwell rather upon excellencies than imperfections, to discover the concealed beauties of a writer, and communicate to the world such things as are worth their observation.

The Spectator, No. 291
February 2, 1712

ISAAC WATTS
(1674-1748)

Were I so tall to reach the pole,
   Or grasp the ocean with my span,
I must be measured by my soul:
   The mind's the standard of the man.

Horae Lyricae (1706). Book II
False Greatness

Let dogs delight to bark and bite,
   For God hath made them so;
Let bears and lions growl and fight,
   For 'tis their nature too.

Divine Songs (1715) XVI

But, children, you should never let
   Such angry passions rise;
Your little hands were never made
   To tear each other's eyes.

Divine Songs (1715) XVI

Joy to the world! the Lord is come;
Let earth receive her King.
Let ev'ry heart prepare Him room,
And heav'n and nature sing.

Psalm XCVIII (1719) Stanza I

WILLIAM SOMERVILLE
(1675-1742)

How humble, and how complaisant
Is the proud man reduced to want!
With what a silly, hanging face
He bears his unforeseen disgrace!

Ready Money (1727)

Let all the learned say what they can,
'Tis ready money makes the man.

Ready Money (1727)

There is something in a face,
An air, and a peculiar grace,
Which boldest painters cannot trace.

The Lucky Hit (1727)

EDWARD YOUNG
(1683-1765)

Be wise with speed;
A fool at forty is a fool indeed.

Love of Fame (1725-1728)
Satire II, Line 282

Procrastination is the thief of time.

Night Thoughts. Night I, Line 393

All men think all men mortal but themselves.

Night Thoughts. Night I, Line 424

Whose yesterdays look backwards with a smile.

Night Thoughts. Night II, Line 334

SAMUEL MADDEN
(1686-1765)

In an orchard there should be enough to eat, enough to lay up,
enough to be stolen, and enough to rot upon the ground.

Quoted by Samuel Johnson
(1783) (Boswell's Life, Vol. II
Page 456, Everyman edition)

HENRY CAREY
(1687?-1743)

Namby Pamby's little rhymes,
Little jingle, little chimes.

Namby Pamby

God save our gracious king!
Long live our noble king!
  God save the king!

God Save the King (1740?)

JOHN GAY
(1688-1732)

When we risk no contradiction,
It prompts the tongue to deal in fiction.

Fables, Part I (1727)
The Elephant and the Bookseller

Is there no hope? the sick man said;
The silent doctor shook his head.

Fables, Part I (1727)
The Sick Man and the Angel

While there is life there's hope, he cried.

Fables, Part I (1727)
The Sick Man and the Angel

Those who in quarrels interpose
Must often wipe a bloody nose.

Fables, Part I (1727)
The Mastiffs

I hate the man who builds his name
On ruins of another's fame.

Fables, Part I (1727)
The Poet and the Rose

Life is a jest, and all things sow it;
I thought so once, but now I know it.

My Own Epitaph

ALEXANDER POPE
(1688-1744)

Music resembles poetry; in each
Are nameless graces which no methods teach,
And which a master-hand alone can reach.
Essay on Criticism, Part I, Line 143

A little learning is a dangerous thing;
Drink deep, or taste not the Pierian spring:
There shallow draughts intoxicate the brain,
And drinking largely sobers us again.
Essay on Criticism, Part II, Line 15

Some praise at morning what they blame at night,
But always think the last opinion right.
Essay on Criticism, Part II, Line 230

To err is human, to forgive divine.
Essay on Criticism, Part II, Line 325

Be silent always when you doubt your sense.
Essay on Criticism, Part III, Line 6

For fools rush in where angels fear to tread.
Essay on Criticism, Part III, Line 53

But when to mischief mortals bend their will,
How soon they find fit instruments of ill!
The Rape of the Lock
Canto III, Line 125

Charms strike the sight, but merit wins the soul.
The Rape of the Lock
Canto V, Line 34

Curse on all laws but those which love has made!
Love, free as air at sight of human ties,
Spreads his light wings, and in a moment flies.
Eloisa to Abelard (1717) Line 74

'Tis education forms the common mind:
Just as the twig is bent the tree's inclined.
Moral Essays (1720-1735)
Epistle I (1733), Line 149

Blessed is he who expects nothing, for he shall never be disappointed.

Letter to Gay (October 6, 1727)

Hope springs eternal in the human breast:
Man never is, but always to be, blest.

Essay on Man, Epistle I, Line 95

Seas roll to waft me, suns to light me rise;
My footstool earth, my canopy the skies.

Essay on Man, Epistle I, Line 139

The learn'd is happy Nature to explore,
The fool is happy that he knows no more;
The rich is happy in the plenty giv'n,
The poor contents him with the care of Heav'n.

Essay on Man, Epistle II, Line 263

Unlearn'd, he knew no schoolman's subtle art,
No language but the language of the heart.

Epistle to Dr. Arbuthnot
Prologue to the Satires, Line 398

I've often wish'd that I had clear,
For life, six hundred pounds a year;
A handsome house to lodge a friend,
A river at my garden's end,
A terrace walk, and half a rood
Of land set out to plant a wood.

Satires, Epistles, and Odes of Horace
Satire VI, Book II, Line 1

Give me again my hollow tree,
A crust of bread, and liberty.

Satires, Epistles, and Odes of Horace
Satire VI, Book II, Line 220

A man should never be ashamed to own he has been in the wrong, which is but saying, in other words, that he is wiser today than he was yesterday.

Thoughts on Various Subjects (1741)

It is with narrow-souled people as with narrow-necked bottles; the less they have in them the more noise they make in pouring out.

Thoughts on Various Subjects (1741)

PHILIP DORMER STANHOPE
EARL OF CHESTERFIELD
(1694-1773)

Whatever is worth doing at all, is worth doing well.

Letters. March 10, 1746

The knowledge of the world is only to be acquired in the world, not in a closet.

Letters. October 4, 1746

An injury is much sooner forgotten than an insult.

Letters. October 9, 1746

Wear your learning, like your watch, in a private pocket: and do not pull it out and strike it, merely to show that you have one.

Letters. February 22, 1748

Idleness is only the refuge of weak minds.

. Letters. July 20, 1749

VOLTAIRE
(FRANCOIS MARIE AROUET)
(1694-1778)

Virtue debases itself in justifying itself.

Oedipe (1718), Act I, Sc. 4

It is better to risk saving a guilty person than to condemn an innocent one.

Zadig (1747), Chap. 6

This agglomeration which was called and which still calls itself the Holy Roman Empire is neither holy, nor Roman, nor an Empire.

Essai sur les Moeurs (1756)

If this is the best of all possible worlds, what then are the others?

Candide, Chap. 6

Optimism, said Candide, is a mania for maintaining that all is well when things are going badly.

Candide, Chap. 19

For what end, then, has this world been formed? . . . . To plague us to death.

Candide, Chap. 21

Common sense is not so common.

*Dictionnaire Philosophique
(1764), Self-love*

In general, the art of government consists in taking as much money as possible from one class of citizens to give to the other.

Dictionnaire Philosophique, Money

If God did not exist, it would be necessary to invent him.

*Epitre a l'Auteur du Livre des
Trois Imposteurs (November 10, 1770)*

I disapprove of what you say, but I will defend to the death your right to say it.

Attributed to Voltaire

JOHN DYER
(1699-1758)

A little rule, a little sway,
A sunbeam in a winter's day,
Is all the proud and mighty have
Between the cradle and the grave.

Grongar Hill (1726), Line 89

JONATHAN EDWARDS
(1703-1758)

Resolved, never to do anything which I should be afraid to do if it were the last hour of my life.

Seventy Resolutions

I assert that nothing ever comes to pass without a cause.

The Freedom of the Will (1754)

JOHN WESLEY
(1703-1791)

I look upon the world as my parish.

Journal. June 11, 1739

Though I am always in haste, I am never in a hurry.
Letters. December 10, 1777

Do all the good you can,
By all the means you can,
In all the ways you can,
In all the places you can,
At all the times you can,
To all the people you can,
As long as ever you can.

John Wesley's Rule

BENJAMIN FRANKLIN
(1706-1790)

Remember that time is money.
Advice to a Young Tradesman (1748)

God helps them that help themselves.
Maxims prefixed to Poor Richard's Almanac
(1757)

Dost thou love life? Then do not squander time, for that is the stuff life is made of.
Maxims prefixed to Poor Richard's Almanac
(1757)

Early to bed and early to rise,
Makes a man healthy, wealthy, and wise.
Maxims prefixed to Poor Richard's Almanac
(1757)

Plough deep while sluggards sleep.
Maxims prefixed to Poor Richard's Almanac
(1757)

Never leave that till tomorrow which you can do today.
Maxims prefixed to Poor Richard's Almanac
(1757)

Little strokes fell great oaks.
Maxims prefixed to Poor Richard's Almanac
(1757)

A little neglect may breed mischief: for want of a nail the shoe was lost; for want of a shoe the horse was lost; and for want of a horse the rider was lost.

Maxims prefixed to Poor Richard's Almanac
(1757)

It is hard for an empty sack to stand upright.

Maxims prefixed to Poor Richard's Almanac
(1757)

They that can give up essential liberty to obtain a little temporary safety deserve neither liberty nor safety.

Historical Review of Pennsylvania (1759)

Her Skugg lies snug
As a bug in a rug.

Letter to Miss Georgiana Shipley
(September, 1772)

There never was a good war or a bad peace.

Letter to Josiah Quincy
(September 11, 1773)

We must all hang together, or assuredly we shall all hang separately.

At the signing of the Declaration of Independence
(July 4, 1776)

I wish the bald eagle had not been chosen as the representative of our country; he is a bird of bad moral character; like those among men who live by sharping and robbing, he is generally poor, and often very lousy.

The turkey is a much more respectable bird, and withal a true original native of America.

Letter to Sarah Bache
(January 26, 1784)

Our Constitution is in actual operation; everything appears to promise that it will last; but in this world nothing is certain but death and taxes.

Letter to M. Leroy (1789)

HENRY FIELDING
(1707-1754)

The dusky night rides down the sky,

And ushers in the morn;
The hounds all join in glorious cry,
The huntsman winds his horn,
And a-hunting we will go.

> *A-Hunting We Will Go (1734)*
> *Stanza I*

Distinction without a difference.

> *The History of Tom Jones (1749)*
> *Book VI, Chap. 13*

When widows exclaim loudly against second marriages, I would always lay a wager that the man, if not the wedding-day, is absolutely fixed on.

> *Amelia (1751) Book VI, Chap. 8*

There is not in the universe a more ridiculous, nor a more contemptible animal, than a proud clergyman.

> *Amelia (1751) Book VI, Chap. 10*

WILLIAM PITT,
EARL OF CHATHAM
(1708-1778)

I rejoice that America has resisted. Three million of people, so dead to all the feelings of liberty, as voluntarily to submit to be slaves, would have been fit instruments to make slaves of the rest.

> *Speech in the House of Commons*
> *March 6, 1741*

Unlimited power is apt to corrupt the minds of those who possess it.

> *Case of Wilkes. Speech*
> *(January 9, 1770)*

Where law ends, tyranny begins.

> *Case of Wilkes. Speech*
> *(January 9, 1770)*

The poorest man may in his cottage bid defiance to all the force of the Crown. It may be frail; its roof may shake; the wind may blow through it; the storms may enter, the rain may enter,—but

the King of England cannot enter; all his forces dare not cross
the threshold of the ruined tenement!

Speech on the Excise Bill

SAMUEL JOHNSON
(1709-1784)

Curiosity is one of the permanent and certain characteristics of
a vigorous mind.

The Rambler (March 12, 1751)

Gratitude is a fruit of great cultivation; you do not find it among
gross people.

Boswell's Tour to the Hebrides
(Published 1785). (Sept. 20, 1773)

Dictionaries are like watches; the worst is better than none, and
the best cannot be expected to go quite true.

Mrs. Piozzi: Anecdotes of Samuel Johnson

Boswell. That, Sir, was great fortitude of mind.
Johnson. No, Sir; stark insensibility.

Boswell's Life of Dr. Johnson
(1791). Vol. I, Page 28

On clean-shirt-day he went abroad, and paid visits.

Boswell's Life of Dr. Johnson
Vol. I, Page 56

If a man does not make new acquaintances as he advances
through life, he will soon find himself left alone. A man, sir,
should keep his friendship in a constant repair.

Boswell's Life of Dr. Johnson
Vol. I, Page 182

Every man's affairs, however little, are important to himself.

Boswell's Life of Dr. Johnson
Vol. I, Page 235

A man of genius has been seldom ruined but by himself.

Boswell's Life of Dr. Johnson
Vol. I, Page 236

If he does really think that there is no distinction between vir-

tue and vice, why, sir, when he leaves our houses let us count
our spoons ·

Boswell's Life of Dr. Johnson
Vol. I, Page 268

If I accustom a servant to tell a lie for *me,* have I not reason to
apprehend that he will tell many lies for *himself?*

Boswell's Life of Dr. Johnson
Vol. I, Page 270

Patriotism is the last refuge of a scoundrel.

Boswell's Life of Dr. Johnson
Vol. I, Page 547

Life is very short, and very uncertain; let us spend it as well as
we can.

Boswell's Life of Dr. Johnson
Vol. II, Page 583

JEAN JACQUES ROUSSEAU
(1712-1778)

Never exceed your rights, and they will soon become unlimited.

A Discourse on Political Economy (1758)

Man is born free, and everywhere he is in chains.

Contrat Social (1762)
Book I, Chap. I

God makes all things good; man meddles with them and they
become evil.

Emile, ou De l'Education (1762)
Book I

People who know little are usually great talkers, while men who
know much say little.

Emile, ou De l'Education
Book I

The happiest is he who suffers least; the most miserable is he
who enjoys least. Ever more sorrow than joy,—this is the lot of
all of us.

Emile, ou De l'Education
Book II

Nature never deceives us; it is always we who deceive ourselves.

Emile, ou De l'Education
Book III

LAURENCE STERNE
(1713-1768)

Only the brave know how to forgive.
... A coward never forgave; it is not in his nature.

Sermons. Vol. I (1760), No. 12

'Tis known by the name of perseverance in a good cause,—and of obstinacy in a bad one.

Tristram Shandy, Book I (1760)
Chap. 17

Persuasion hung upon his lips.

Tristram Shandy, Book I (1760)
Chap. 19

DAVID GARRICK
(1716-1779)

Let others hail the rising sun:
I bow to that whose course is run.

On the Death of Mr. Pelham

Heart of oak are our ships,
Heart of oak are our men,
  We always are ready,
  Steady, boys, steady,
We'll fight, and we'll conquer again and again.

Heart of Oak (Circa 1770)

THOMAS GRAY
(1716-1771)

The curfew tolls the knell of parting day,
The lowing herd wind slowly o'er the lea,
The ploughman homeward plods his weary way,

And leaves the world to darkness and to me.
Elegy in a Country Churchyard
(1750) Stanza I

The boast of heraldry, the pomp of pow'r
And all that beauty, all that wealth e'er gave,
Await alike the inevitable hour:
The paths of glory lead but to the grave.
Elegy in a Country Churchyard
Stanza 9

HORACE WALPOLE
(1717-1797)

The world is a comedy to those that think, a tragedy to those
that feel.
Letter to Sir Horace Mann (1769)

Prognostics do not always prove prophecies,—at least the
wisest prophets make sure of the event first.
Letter to Thomas Walpole (1785)

ADAM SMITH
(1723-1790)

The real price of everything, what everything really costs to the
man who wants to acquire it, is the toil and trouble of acquiring
it.
Wealth of Nations (1776)

To found a great empire for the sole purpose of raising up a
people of customers may at first sight appear a project fit only
for a nation of shopkeepers. It is, however, a project altogether
unfit for a nation of shopkeepers; but extremely fit for a nation
whose Government is influenced by shopkeepers.
Wealth of Nations

WILLIAM PRESCOTT
(1726-1795)

Don't fire until you see the whites of their eyes.
At Bunker Hill, June 17, 1775

OLIVER GOLDSMITH
(1728-1774)

We sometimes had those little rubs which Providence sends to enhance the value of its favours.

The Vicar of Wakefield (1766)
Chap. I

When lovely woman stoops to folly,
And finds too late that men betray,
What charm can soothe her melancholy?
What art can wash her guilt away?

The Vicar of Wakefield, Chap. 24
An Elegy on the Death of a Mad Dog
Stanza I

The only art her guilt to cover,
To hide her shame from every eye,
To give repentance to her lover,
And wring his bosom, is—to die.

The Vicar of Wakefield, Chap. 24
An Elegy on the Death of a Mad Dog
Stanza 2

Silence gives consent.

The Good-Natur'd Man (1768), Act II

The bashful virgin's sidelong looks of love.

The Deserted Village (1770), Line 29

His best companions, innocence and health;
And his best riches, ignorance of wealth.

The Deserted Village (1770), Line 61

Thou source of all my bliss and all my woe,
That found'st me poor at first, and keep'st me so.

The Deserted Village, Line 413

The very pink of perfection.

She Stoops to Conquer (1773)
Act I

Let schoolmasters puzzle their brain,
  With grammar, and nonsense, and learning;

Good liquor, I stoutly maintain,
  Gives genius a better discerning.
She Stoops to Conquer (1773)
Act I

Ask me no questions, and I'll tell you no fibs.
She Stoops to Conquer, Act III

The very pink of courtesy and circumspection.
She Stoops to Conquer, Act IV

He cast off his friends, as a huntsman his pack,
For he knew when he pleas'd he could whistle them back.
Retaliation, Line 107

I consider an author's literary reputation to be alive only while his name will insure a good price for his copy from the bookseller's.
Boswell's Life of Dr. Johnson
(1791). Vol. I, Page 468
Everyman Edition

JOHN PARKER
(1729-1775)

Stand your ground. Don't fire unless fired upon; but if they mean to have a war, let it begin here!
To his Minute Men at Lexington
April 19, 1775

EDMUND BURKE
(1729-1797)

The writers against religion, whilst they oppose every system, are wisely careful never to set up any of their own.
A Vindication of Natural Society
(1756)

I am convinced that we have a degree of delight, and that no small one, in the real misfortunes and pains of others.
On the Sublime and Beautiful
(1756). Sect. XIV

Reflect how you are to govern a people who think they ought to be free, and think they are not. Your scheme yields no revenue; it yields nothing but discontent, disorder, disobedience; and such is the state of America, that after wading up to your eyes in blood, you could only end just where you begun; that is, to tax where no revenue is to be found, to—my voice fails me; my inclination indeed carries me no farther—all is confusion beyond it.

First Speech on Conciliation with America
American Taxation (April 19, 1774)

The use of force alone is but *temporary*. It may subdue for a moment; but it does not remove the necessity of subduing again: and a nation is not governed, which is perpetually to be conquered.

Second Speech on Conciliation with America
The Thirteen Resolutions

It is not, what a lawyer tells me I *may* do; but what humanity, reason, and justice, tell me I ought to do.

Second Speech on Conciliation with America
The Thirteen Resolutions

The march of the human mind is slow.

Second Speech on Conciliation with America
The Thirteen Resolutions

Freedom and not servitude is the cure of anarchy; as religion, and not atheism, is the true remedy for superstition.

Second Speech on Conciliation with America
The Thirteen Resolutions

He was not merely a chip of the old block, but the old block itself.

On Pitt's First Speech (February 26, 1781).
From Wraxall's Memoirs, First Series, Vol. I, Page 342

The people never give up their liberties but under some delusion.

Speech at County Meeting of
Buckinghamshire (1784)

Because half-a-dozen grasshoppers under a fern make the field ring with their importunate chink, whilst thousands of great cattle, reposed beneath the shadow of the British oak, chew the cud and are silent, pray do not imagine that those who make

the noise are the only inhabitants of the field; that of course
they are many in number; or that, after all, they are other than
the little shrivelled, meagre, hopping, though loud and
troublesome insects of the hour.

Reflections on the Revolution in France

I would rather sleep in the southern corner of a little country
churchyard than in the tomb of the Capulets

Letter of Matthew Smith

JOHN SCOTT
(1730-1783)

I hate that drum's discordant sound,
Parading round, and round, and round:
To me it talks of ravaged plains,
And burning towns, and ruined swains,
And mangled limbs, and dying groans,
And widows' tears, and orphans' moans;
And all that Misery's hand bestows
To fill the catalogue of human woes.

I Hate That Drum's Discordant Sound
Stanza 2

WILLIAM COWPER
(1731-1800)

What peaceful hours I once enjoy'd!
    How sweet their memory still!
But they have left an aching void
    The world can never fill.

Olney Hymns (1779)
Walking with God

God moves in a mysterious way
    His wonders to perform;
He plants his footsteps in the sea
    And rides upon the storm.

Olney Hymns (1779)
Light Shining out of Darkness

Behind a frowning providence
He hides a shining face.

Olney Hymns (1779)
Light Shining out of Darkness

Knowledge is proud that he has learn'd so much;
Wisdom is humble that he knows no more.

The Task, Book VI, Winter Walk
at Noon, Line 96

GEORGE WASHINGTON
(1732-1799)

Labour to keep alive in your breast that little spark of celestial
fire,—conscience.

Rule from the copybook of
Washington when a schoolboy.
Jared Sparks' Life of Washington
(1839), Vol. II, Page 109

If men are to be precluded from offering their sentiments on a
matter, which may involve the most serious and alarming con-
sequences that can invite the consideration of mankind, reason
is of no use to us; the freedom of speech may be taken away,
and dumb and silent we may be led, like sheep to the slaughter.

Address to Officers of the Army
(March 15, 1783)

Almighty God, we make our earnest prayer that Thou wilt keep
the United States in Thy holy protection; that Thou wilt incline
the hearts of the citizens to cultivate a spirit of subordination
and obedience to government; to entertain a brotherly affec-
tion and love for one another and for their fellow-citizens of
the United States at large.

Prayer after Inauguration (1789)

There can be no greater error than to expect or calculate upon
real favors from nation to nation.

First Annual Address, to both
Houses of Congress (January 8, 1790)

JOHN ADAMS
(1735-1826)

All great changes are irksome to the human mind, especially those which are attended with great dangers and uncertain effects.

Letter to James Warren
(April 22, 1776)

Yesterday the greatest question was decided which ever was debated in America; and a greater perhaps never was, nor will be, decided among men. A resolution was passed without one dissenting colony, that these United Colonies are, and of right ought to be, free and independent States.

Letter to Abigail Adams
(July 3, 1776)

The second day of July, 1776, will be the most memorable epoch in the history of America. I am apt to believe that it will be celebrated by succeeding generations as the great anniversary festival. It ought to be commemorated as the day of deliverance, by solemn acts of devotion to God Almighty. It ought to be solemnized with pomp and parade, with shows, games, sports, guns, bells, bonfires, and illuminations, from one end of this continent to the other, from this time forward for evermore.

Letter to Abigail Adams
(July 3, 1776)

JOHN LANGHORNE
(1735-1779)

The child of misery, baptized in tears.

The Country Justice, Part I

PATRICK HENRY
(1736-1799)

I have but one lamp by which my feet are guided, and that is the lamp of experience. I know no way of judging of the future but by the past.

Speech in Virginia Convention,
St. John's Episcopal Church,
Richmond, Virginia (March 23, 1775)

We are not weak if we make a proper use of those means which the God of Nature has placed in our power . . . . The battle, sir, is not to the strong alone; it is to the vigilant, the active, the brave.

Speech in Virginia Convention,
St. John's Episcopal Church,
Richmond, Virginia

Is life so dear, or peace so sweet, as to be purchased at the price of chains and slavery? Forbid it, Almighty God! I know not what course others may take, but as for me, give me liberty, or give me death!

Speech in Virginia Convention,
St. John's Episcopal Church,
Richmond, Virginia

RUDOLF ERICH RASPE
(1737-1794)

What in the dark I had taken to be a stump of a little tree appearing above the snow, to which I had tied my horse, proved to have been the weathercock of the church steeple.

Travels of Baron Munchausen
(1785), Chap. 2

I have ever confined myself to facts.

Travels of Baron Munchausen
Chap. 20

A traveller has a right to relate and embellish his adventures as he pleases, and it is very unpolite to refuse that deference and applause they deserve.

Travels of Baron Munchausen
Chap. 21

There is a right and wrong handle to everything.

Travels of Baron Munchausen
Chap. 30

THOMAS PAINE
(1737-1809)

From the east to the west blow the trumpets to arms!
Through the land let the sound of it flee;
Let the far and the near all unite, with a cheer,
In defence of our Liberty Tree.

The Liberty Tree (July, 1775)
Stanza 4

These are the times that try men's souls. The summer soldier and the sunshine patriot will, in this crisis, shrink from the service of his country; but he that stands it *now*, deserves the love and thanks of man and woman. Tyranny, like hell, is not easily conquered; yet we have this consolation with us, that the harder the conflict, the more glorious the triumph. What we obtain too cheap, we esteem too lightly; 'tis dearness only that gives everything its value. Heaven knows how to put a proper price upon its goods; and it would be strange indeed, if so celestial an article as *Freedom* should not be highly rated.

The American Crisis, No. I
(December 23, 1776)

Those who expect to reap the blessings of freedom must, like men, undergo the fatigue of supporting it.

The American Crisis, No. IV
(September 12, 1777)

I believe in one God and no more, and I hope for happiness beyond this life. I believe in the equality of man; and I believe that religious duties consist in doing justice, loving mercy, and endeavoring to make our fellow-creatures happy.

The Age of Reason (1793), Part I

THOMAS JEFFERSON
(1743-1826)

The God who gave us life, gave us liberty at the same time.

Summary View of the Rights
of British America (1774)

When, in the course of human events, it becomes necessary for one people to dissolve the political bands which have connected them with another, and to assume among the powers of the earth the separate and equal station to which the laws of nature and of nature's God entitle them, a decent respect to the opinions of mankind requires that they should declare the causes which impel them to the separation. We hold these truths to be self-evident; that all men are created equal; that they are endowed by their creator with certain unalienable rights; that among these are life, liberty, and the pursuit of happiness; that to secure these rights, governments are instituted among men, deriving their just powers from the consent of the governed; that whenever any form of government becomes destructive to these ends, it is the right of the people to alter or to abolish it, and to institute new government, laying its foundation on such principles, and organizing its powers in such form, as to them shall seem most likely to effect their safety and happiness.

Declaration of Independence
(July 4, 1776)

He who permits himself to tell a lie once, finds it much easier to do it a second and third time, till at length it becomes habitual; he tells lies without attending to it, and truths without the world's believing him. This falsehood of the tongue leads to that of the heart, and in time depraves all its good dispositions.

Letter to Peter Carr
(August 19, 1785)

I hold it, that a little rebellion, now and then, is a good thing, and as necessary in the political world as storms in the physical.

Letter to James Madison
(January 30, 1787)

. . . The tree of liberty must be refreshed from time to time with the blood of patriots and tyrants. It is its natural manure.

Letter to William Stevens Smith
(November 13, 1787)

I have sworn upon the altar of God, eternal hostility against every form of tyranny over the mind of man.

Letter to Dr. Benjamin Rush
(September 23, 1800)

The earth belongs to the living, not to the dead.

Letter to John W. Eppes
(June 24, 1813)

Never buy what you do not want, because it is cheap; it will be dear to you.

A Decalogue of Canons for
Observation in Practical Life
(February 21, 1825)

When angry, count ten before you speak; if very angry, an hundred.

A Decalogue of Canons for
Observation in Practical Life
(February 21, 1825)

JAMES HOOK
(1746-1827)

A little farm well tilled,
A little barn well filled,
A little wife well willed,
   Give me, give me.

The Soldier's Return, Stanza 1

I like the farm well tilled,
And I like the house well filled,
But no wife at all
   Give me, give me.

The Soldier's Return, Stanza 3

CHARLES COTESWORTH PINCKNEY
(1746-1825)

Millions for defence, but not one cent for tribute.

When Minister to the
French Republic (1797)

JOHN PAUL JONES
(1742-1792)

I have not yet begun to fight.

Aboard the Bonhomme Richard

JOHN O'KEEFFE
(1747-1833)

A glass is good, and a lass is good,
  And a pipe to smoke in cold weather;
The world is good, and the people are good,
  And we're all good fellows together.

Sprigs of Laurel. Act II, Sc. 1

JOHN LOGAN
(1748-1788)

Thou hast no sorrow in thy song,
  No winter in thy year.

To the Cuckoo

Oh could I fly, I'd fly with thee!
  We'd make with joyful wing
Our annual visit o'er the globe,
  Companions of the spring.

To the Cuckoo

JOHN EDWIN
(1749-1790)

A man's ingress into the world is naked and bare,
His progress through the world is trouble and care;
And lastly, his egress out of the world, is nobody
  knows where.
If we do well here, we shall do well there:
I can tell you no more if I preach a whole year.

The Eccentricities of John Edwin
(second edition, London, 1791)
Vol. I, Page 74

JOHANN WOLFGANG VON GOETHE
(1749-1832)

If you inquire what the people are like here, I must answer,

"The same as everywhere!"

The Sorrows of Werther
(1774-1787) May 17th

Who never ate his bread in sorrow,
  Who never spent the darksome hours
Weeping, and watching for the morrow,—
  He knows you not, ye heavenly
    Powers.

Wilhelm Meister's Apprenticeship
(1786-1830) Book II, Chap. 13

One ought, every day at least, to hear a little song, read a good poem, see a fine picture, and, if it were possible, to speak a few reasonable words.

Wilhelm Meister's Apprenticeship
(1786-1830) Book V, Chap. I

To know of some one here and there whom we accord with, who is living on with us, even in silence,—this makes our earthly ball a peopled garden.

Wilhelm Meister's Apprenticeship
(1786-1830) Book VII, Chap. 5

Art is long, life short; judgment difficult, opportunity transient.

Wilhelm Meister's Apprenticeship
(1786-1830) Book VII, Chap. 9

JAMES MADISON
(1751-1836)

To secure the public good, and private rights, against the danger of . . . faction, and at the same time to preserve the spirit and form of popular government, is then the great object to which our inquiries are directed.

The Federalist (1787-1788)

JOHANN HENRICH VOSS
(1751-1826)

Who does not love wine, women, and song
Remains a fool his whole life long.

Couplet

BERTRAND BARERE
(1755-1841)

The tree of liberty only grows when watered by the blood of tyrants.

Speech in the National Convention (1792)

It is only the dead who do not return.

Speech (1794)

HENRY LEE
(1756-1818)

To the memory of the Man, first in war, first in peace, and first in the hearts of his countrymen.

Resolutions Presented to the
House of Representatives on the
Death of Washington (December, 1799)

WILLIAM BLAKE
(1757-1827)

Does the eagle know what is in the pit?
Or wilt thou go ask the mole?
Can Wisdom be put in a silver rod?
Or Love in a golden bowl?

The Book of Thel (1789)
Thel's Motto

Little Lamb, who made thee?
Dost thou know who made thee?
Gave thee life, and bid thee feed
By the stream and o'er the mead;
Gave thee clothing of delight,
Softest clothing, woolly, bright.

Songs of Innocence (1789)
The Lamb, Stanza I

Can I see another's woe,
And not be in sorrow too?

Can I see another's grief,
And not seek for kind relief?

Songs of Innocence
On Another's Sorrow,
Stanza I

The weak in courage is strong in cunning.

The Marriage of Heaven and Hell
Proverbs of Hell

I asked a thief to steal me a peach:
He turned up his eyes.
I ask'd a lithe lady to lie her down:
Holy and meek she cries.

As soon as I went an angel came:
He wink'd at the thief
And smil'd at the dame,
And without one word spoke
Had a peach from the tree,
And 'twixt earnest and joke
Enjoy'd the Lady.

Poems from MSS. (Circa 1793)
Untitled Poem

Little Fly,
Thy summer's play
My thoughtless hand
Has brush'd away.

Songs of Experience
The Fly, Stanza I

In every cry of every man,
In every infant's cry of fear,
In every voice, in every ban,
The mind-forg'd manacles I hear.

Songs of Experience
London, Stanza 2

A robin redbreast in a cage
Puts all Heaven in a rage.

Poems (Circa 1803)
Auguries of Innocence, Line 5

ROBERT BURNS
(1759-1796)

When chill November's surly blast
Made fields and forests bare.

Man Was Made to Mourn
(1786) Stanza I

Man's inhumanity to man
Makes countless thousands mourn.

Man Was Made to Mourn
(1786) Stanza 7

Should auld acquaintance be forgot,
And never brought to mind?
Should auld acquaintance be forgot,
And auld lang syne!

Auld Lang Syne (1788) Stanza I

For auld lang syne, my dear,
For auld lang syne,
We'll tak a cup o'kindness yet
For auld lang syne!

Auld Lang Syne (1788) Chorus

She is a winsome wee thing,
She is a handsome wee thing,
She is a lo'esome wee thing,
This sweet wee wife o' mine.

My Wife's a Winsome Wee Thing
(1792) Chorus

JOHANN CHRISTOPH FRIEDRICH VON SCHILLER
(1759-1805)

There are three lessons I would write,
Three words as with a burning pen,
In tracings of eternal light,
Upon the hearts of men.

Hope, Faith, and Love, Stanza I

When the wine goes in, strange things come out.
The Piccolomini (1799)
Act II, Sc. 12

Against stupidity the very gods
Themselves contend in vain.
The Maid of Orleans (1801)
Act III, Sc. 6

JOHN QUINCY ADAMS
(1767-1848)

Think of your forefathers! Think of your posterity!
Speech at Plymouth
(December 22, 1802)

In charity to all mankind, bearing no malice or ill-will to any human being, and even compassionating those who hold in bondage their fellow-men, not knowing what they do.
Letter to A. Bronson
(July 30, 1838)

NAPOLEON BONAPARTE
(1769-1821)

Soldiers, from the summit of yonder pyramids forty centuries look down upon you.
In Egypt (July 21, 1798)

From the sublime to the ridiculous is but a step.
To the Abbe du Pradt, on the return
from Russia (1812), referring
to the retreat from Moscow

The bullet that will kill me is not yet cast.
At Montereau (February 17, 1814)

Our hour is marked, and no one can claim a moment of life beyond what fate has predestined.
To Dr. Arnott (April, 1821)

ARTHUR WELLESLEY
DUKE OF WELLINGTON
(1769-1852)

Nothing except a battle lost can be half so melancholy as a battle won.

Dispatch (1815)

There is no mistake; there has been no mistake; and there shall be no mistake.

Letter to Mr. Huskisson

I care not one twopenny damn.

Quoted in George Otto Trevelyan:
Life and Letters of Lord Macaulay
(1876), Vol. II, Page 221

The battle of Waterloo was won on the playing fields of Eton.

Quoted in Fraser,
Words on Wellington (1889)

DAVID EVERETT
(1770-1813)

You'd scarce expect one of my age
To speak in public on the stage;
And if I chance to fall below
Demosthenes or Cicero,
Don't view me with a critic's eye,
But pass my imperfections by.
Large streams from little fountains flow,
Tall oaks from little acorns grow.

Lines written for a school declamation
for Ephraim H. Farrar, aged seven,
New Ipswich, New Hampshire (1791)

GEORG WILHELM FRIEDRICH HEGEL
(1770-1831)

Peoples and governments never have learned anything from

history, or acted on principles deduced from it.

Philosophy of History (1832)
Introduction

The history of the world is none other than the progress of the consciousness of freedom.

Philosophy of History
Introduction

It is a matter of perfect indifference where a thing originated; the only question is: "Is it true in and for itself?"

Philosophy of History
Part III, Sect. 3, Chap. 2

When liberty is mentioned, we must always be careful to observe whether it is not really the assertion of private interests which is thereby designated.

Philosophy of History
Part IV, Sect. 3, Chap. 2

The Few assume to be the *deputies,* but they are often only the *despoilers* of the Many.

Philosophy of History
Part IV, Sect. 3, Chap. 3

WILLIAM ROBERT SPENCER
(1770-1834)

When the black-lettered list to the gods was presented,
(The list of what Fate for each mortal intends,)
At the long string of ills a kind goddess relented,
And slipped in three blessings—wife, children and friends.

Wife, Children, and Friends
Stanza I

WILLIAM WORDSWORTH
(1770-1850)

Come forth into the light of things,
Let Nature be your teacher.

The Tables Turned (1798)
Stanza 4

There's not a man
That lives who hath not known his god-like hours.
The Prelude (Written 1799-1805)
Book III

How men lived
Even next-door neighbours, as we say, yet still
Strangers, not knowing each the other's name.
The Prelude, Book VII

Three years she grew in sun and shower,
Then Nature said, "A lovelier flower
On earth was never sown;
This Child I to myself will take;
She shall be mine, and I will make
A Lady of my own."
Lucy: Three Years She Grew in Sun
and Shower (1799), Stanza I

Who is the happy Warrior? Who is he
That every man in arms would wish to be?
Character of the Happy Warrior
(1806)

The world is too much with us; late and soon,
Getting and spending, we lay waste our powers:
Little we see in Nature that is ours.
The World Is Too Much With Us
(1806)

Strongest minds
Are often those of whom the noisy world
Hears least.
The Excursion (Published 1814)
Book I

Wrongs unredressed, or insults unavenged.
The Excursion (Published 1814)
Book III

Society became my glittering bride.
The Excursion (Published 1814)
Book III

A man he seems of cheerful yesterdays
And confident tomorrows.

The Excursion, Book VII

Minds that have nothing to confer
Find little to perceive.

Yes, Thou art Fair (1845)
Stanza 2

THOMAS DIBDIN
(1771-1841)

Oh, it's a snug little island
A right little, tight little island.

The Snug Little Island

JAMES MONTGOMERY
(1771-1854)

Tomorrow—oh, 'twill never be,
If we should live a thousand years!
Our time is all today, today.

Today

Give me the hand that is honest and hearty,
Free as the breeze and unshackled by party.

Give Me Thy Hand, Stanza 2

The rose has but a summer reign,
The daisy never dies.

The Daisy, Stanza 10

Prayer is the soul's sincere desire,
   Uttered or unexpressed;
The motion of a hidden fire
   That trembles in the breast.

What is Prayer? Stanza I

Prayer is the burden of a sigh,
   The falling of a tear;
The upward glancing of an eye,
   When none but God is near.

What is Prayer? Stanza 2

SIR WALTER SCOTT
(1771-1832)

The way was long, the wind was cold,
The Minstrel was infirm and old;
His withered cheek, and tresses gray,
Seem'd to have known a better day.

The Lay of the Last Minstrel
(1805) Introduction

To all, to each, a fair good-night,
And pleasing dreams, and slumbers light.

Marmion, L'Envoy, To the Reader

Hail to the Chief who in triumph advances!

The Lady of the Lake (1810)
Canto II, Stanza 19

Like the dew on the mountain,
    Like the foam on the river,
Like the bubble on the fountain,
    Thou art gone, and forever!

The Lady of the Lake, Canto III
Stanza 16 (Coronach, Stanza 3)

Come fill up my cup, come fill up my can,
Come saddle your horses, and call up your men;
Come open the West Port, and let me gang free,
And it's room for the bonnets of Bonny Dundee!

The Doom of Devorgoil (1830)
Bonny Dundee, Chorus

One hour of life, crowded to the full with glorious action, and
filled with noble risks, is worth whole years of those mean
observances of paltry decorum.

Count Robert of Paris (1832)
Chap. 25

Heaven knows its time; the bullet has its billet.

Count Robert of Paris (1832)
Chap. 25

SYDNEY SMITH
(1771-1845)

Great men hallow a whole people, and lift up all who live in their time.

Lady Holland's Memoir
Vol. I, Chap. 7

He has spent all his life in letting down empty buckets into empty wells; and he is frittering away his age in trying to draw them up again.

Lady Holland's Memoir
Vol. I, Chap. 9

As the French say, there are three sexes—men, women, and clergymen.

Lady Holland's Memoir
Vol. I, Chap. 9

I have gout, asthma, and seven other maladies, but am otherwise very well.

Lady Holland's Memoir
Vol. I, Chap. 10

He was a one-book man. Some men have only one book in them; others, a library.

Lady Holland's Memoir
Vol. I, Chap. 11

Marriage resembles a pair of shears, so joined that they can not be separated; often moving in opposite directions, yet always punishing anyone who comes between them.

Lady Holland's Memoir
Vol. I, Chap. 11

What you don't know would make a great book.

Lady Holland's Memoir
Recipe for Salad

We know nothing of tomorrow; our business is to be good and happy today.

Lady Holland's Memoir
Recipe for Salad

SAMUEL TAYLOR COLERIDGE
(1772-1834)

Poor little Foal of an oppressed race!
I love the languid patience of thy face.

To a Young Ass (1794)

"God save thee, ancient Mariner!
From fiends, that plague thee thus!—
Why look'st thou so?"—"With my cross-bow
I shot the Albatross."

The Ancient Mariner (1798-1834)
Part I, Stanza 20

As idle as a painted ship
Upon a painted ocean.

The Ancient Mariner
Part II, Stanza 8

Water, water, everywhere,
Nor any drop to drink.

The Ancient Mariner
Part II, Stanza 9

Every reform, however necessary, will by weak minds be carried to an excess, that itself will need reforming.

Biographia Literaria (1817)
Chap. I

Experience informs us that the first defence of weak minds is to recriminate.

Biographia Literaria (1817)
Chap. 2

Our myriad-minded Shakespeare.

Biographia Literaria (1817)
Chap. 15

The infallible test of a blameless style: namely, its untranslatableness in words of the same language, without injury to the meaning.

Biographia Literaria, Chap. 22

Beneath this sod
A poet lies, or that which once seemed he—

Oh, lift a thought in prayer for S.T.C.!
That he, who many a year, with toil of breath,
Found death in life, may here find life in death.

Epitaph written for himself (1833)

JOHN RANDOLPH
(1773-1833)

The surest way to prevent war is not to fear it.

Speech, U.S. House of Representatives
(March 5, 1806)

He is a man of splendid abilities, but utterly corrupt. He shines and stinks like rotten mackerel by moonlight.

Of Edward Livingston

WILLIAM HENRY HARRISON
(1773-1841)

We admit of no government by divine right ... the only legitimate right to govern is an express grant of power from the governed.

Inaugural Address (March 4, 1841)

Never with my consent shall an officer of the people, comp?n-sated for his services out of their pockets, become the pliant in-strument of the Executive will.

Inaugural Address (March 4, 1841)

ROBERT SOUTHEY
(1774-1843)

"You are old, Father William" the young man cried,
"The few locks which are left you are gray;
You are hale, Father William, a hearty old man—
Now tell me the reason I pray."

The Old Man's Comforts and How
He Gained Them, Stanza I

"In the days of my youth," Father William replied,
"I remembered that youth could not last;

I thought of the future, whatever I did,
That I never might grieve for the past."

The Old Man's Comforts and How
He Gained Them, Stanza I

CHARLES LAMB
(1775-1834)

The human species, according to the best theory I can form of
it, is composed of two distinct races, the men who borrow, and
the men who lend.

Essays of Elia (1823)
The Two Races of Men

Borrowers of books—those mutilators of collections, spoilers of
the symmetry of shelves, and creators of odd volumes.

Essays of Elia (1823)
The Two Races of Men

Sentimentally I am disposed to harmony; but organically I am
incapable of a tune.

Essays of Elia, A Chapter on Ears

Books think for me.

Last Essays of Elia (1833)
Detached Thoughts on Books and Reading

Books which are no books.

Last Essays of Elia (1833)
Detached Thoughts on Books and Reading

If there be a regal solitude, it is a sick bed.

Last Essays of Elia (1833)
The Convalescent

How sickness enlarges the dimensions of a man's self to
himself.

Last Essays of Elia (1833)
The Convalescent

Your absence of mind we have borne, till your presence of
body came to be called in question by it.

Last Essays of Elia
Amicus Redivivus

A pun is a pistol let off at the ear; not a feather to tickle the intellect.

Last Essays of Elia
Popular Fallacies: IX, That the
Worst Puns are the Best

A presentation copy . . . is a copy of a book which does not sell, sent you by the author, with his foolish autograph at the beginning of it; for which, if a stranger, he only demands your friendship; if a brother author, he expects from you a book of yours, which does not sell, in return.

Last Essays of Elia
That We Must Not Look a
Gift-Horse in the Mouth

THOMAS CAMPBELL
(1777-1844)

On the green banks of Shannon, when Sheelah was nigh,
No blithe Irish lad was so happy as I;
No harp like my own could so cheerfully play,
And wherever I went was my poor dog Tray.

The Harper (1799), Stanza I

To live in hearts we leave behind
Is not to die.

Hallowed Ground, Stanza 6

HENRY CLAY
(1777-1852)

If you wish to avoid foreign collision, you had better abandon the ocean.

Speech, U.S. House of Representatives
(January 22, 1812)

Government is a trust, and the officers of the government are trustees; and both the trust and the trustees are created for the benefit of the people.

Speech at Ashland, Kentucky
(March, 1829)

Sir, I would rather be right than be President.

Speech (1850)

General Alexander Smyth, a tedious speaker in Congress, observed: "You, sir, speak for the present generation; but I speak for posterity."

"Yes," said Mr. Clay, "and you seem resolved to speak until the arrival of your audience."

*Quoted by Epes Sargent in
Life of Henry Clay*

COLONEL VALENTINE BLACKER
(1778-1823)

Put your trust in God, my boys, and keep your powder dry!

Oliver Cromwell's Advice (1834)

WILLIAM HAZLITT
(1778-1830)

One of the pleasantest things in the world is going a journey; but I like to go by myself.

On Going a Journey

The soul of a journey is liberty, perfect liberty, to think, feel, do just as one pleases.

On Going a Journey

What I mean by living to one's self is living in the world, as in it, not of it . . . It is to be a silent spectator of the mighty scene of things; . . . to take a thoughtful, anxious interest or curiosity in what is passing in the world, but not to feel the slightest inclination to make or meddle with it.

On Living to One's Self

Even in the common affairs of life, in love, friendship, and marriage, how little security have we when we trust our happiness in the hands of others!

On Living to One's Self

No young man believes he shall ever die.

The Feeling of Immortality in Youth

As we advance in life, we acquire a keener sense of the value of time. Nothing else, indeed, seems of any consequence; and we become misers in this respect.

The Feeling of Immortality in Youth

The only true retirement is that of the heart; the only true leisure is the repose of the passions. To such persons it makes little difference whether they are young or old; and they die as they have lived, with graceful resignation.

The Feeling of Immortality in Youth

Men of genius do not excel in any profession because they labour in it, but they labour in it, because they excel.

Characteristics

FRANCIS SCOTT KEY
(1779-1843)

Oh, say can you see by the dawn's early light,
What so proudly we hailed at the twilight's last gleaming?
Whose broad stripes and bright stars, thro' the perilous fight,
O'er the ramparts we watched were so gallantly streaming?
And the rockets' red glare, the bombs bursting in air,
Gave proof thro' the night that our flag was still there.
Oh, say does that star-spangled banner yet wave
O'er the land of the free and the home of the brave?

The Star-Spangled Banner
(September 14, 1814) Stanza I

Then conquer we must, for our cause it is just—
And this be our motto—"In God is our trust!"

The Star-Spangled Banner
(September 14, 1814) Stanza 4

CLEMENT CLARKE MOORE
(1779-1863)

'Twas the night before Christmas, when all through the house
Not a creature was stirring—not even a mouse;
The stockings were hung by the chimney with care,
In hopes that St. Nicholas soon would be there.

A Visit from St. Nicholas
(December, 1823)

"Happy Christmas to all, and to all a good-night!"

A Visit from St. Nicholas
(December, 1823)

CHARLES CALEB COLTON
(1780-1832)

Imitation is the sincerest of flattery.

The Lacon

THOMAS MOORE
(1780-1852)

Weep on! and, as thy sorrows flow,
I'll taste the luxury of woe.

Juvenile Poems, Anacreontic,
Press the Grape, Stanza 2

Row, brothers, row, the stream runs fast,
The rapids are near, and the daylight's past.

Poems Relating to America
A Canadian Boat-Song, Stanza 1

But there's nothing half so sweet in life
As love's young dream.

Irish Melodies. Love's Young
Dream, Stanza 1

'Tis the last rose of summer,
   Left blooming alone;
All her lovely companions
   Are faded and gone;
No flower of her kindred,
   No rosebud is nigh,
To reflect back her blushes,
   Or give sigh for sigh.

Irish Melodies. The Last Rose
of Summer, Stanza 1

Ask a woman's advice, and, whate'er she advise,
Do the very reverse and you're sure to be wise.

Satirical and Humorous Poems
How to Make a Good Politician

JOHN C. CALHOUN
(1782-1850)

The very essence of a free government consists in considering offices as public trusts, bestowed for the good of the country, and not for the benefit of an individual or a party.

Speech (February 13, 1835)

A power has risen up in the government greater than the people themselves, consisting of many and various and powerful interests, combined into one mass, and held together by the cohesive power of the vast surplus in the banks.

Speech (May 27, 1836)

DANIEL WEBSTER
(1782-1852)

Mind is the great lever of all things; human thought is the process by which human ends are ultimately answered.

*Address on Laying the Cornerstone
of the Bunker Hill Monument
(June 17, 1825)*

Knowledge, in truth, is the great sun in the firmament. Life and power are scattered with all its beams.

*Address on Laying the Cornerstone
of the Bunker Hill Monument
(June 17, 1825)*

Let our object be our country, our whole country, and nothing but our country.

*Address on Laying the Cornerstone
of the Bunker Hill Monument
(June 17, 1825)*

Sink or swim, live or die, survive or perish, I give my hand and my heart to this vote.

*Discourse in Commemoration
of Adams and Jefferson, Faneuil
Hall, Boston (August 2, 1826)*

The people's government, made for the people, made by the

people, and answerable to the people.

Second Speech on Foote's Resolution
(January 26, 1830)

When my eyes shall be turned to behold for the last time the sun in heaven, may I not see him shining on the broken and dishonored fragments of a once glorious Union; on States dissevered, discordant, belligerent; on a land rent with civil feuds, or drenched, it may be, in fraternal blood.

Second Speech on Foote's Resolution

Liberty and Union, now and forever, one and inseparable.

Second Speech on Foote's Resolution

There is nothing so powerful as truth—and often nothing so strange.

Argument on the Murder of
Captain White (April 6, 1830)

God grants liberty only to those who love it, and are always ready to guard and defend it.

Speech (June 3, 1834)

I was born an American; I will live an American; I shall die an American.

Speech (July 17, 1850)

WASHINGTON IRVING
(1783-1859)

Who ever hears of fat men heading a riot, or herding together in turbulent mobs?—no—no, 'tis your lean, hungry men who are continually worrying society, and setting the whole community by the ears.

Knickerbocker's History of
New York (1809). Book II, Chap. 3

There is in every true woman's heart a spark of heavenly fire, which lies dormant in the broad daylight of prosperity; but which kindles up, and beams and blazes in the dark hour of adversity.

The Sketch-Book (1819-1820)
The Wife

A sharp tongue is the only edge tool that grows keener with constant use.

The Sketch-Book
Rip Van Winkle

Whenever a man's friends begin to compliment him about looking young, he may be sure that they think he is growing old.

Bracebridge Hall (1822)
Bachelors

HENRI BEYLE (STENDAHL)
(1783-1842)

One can acquire everything in solitude—except character.

Fragments. I

A wise woman never yields by appointment. It should always be an unforeseen happiness.

De l'Amour (1822) Chap. 60

Wit lasts no more than two centuries.

Reply to Balzac. October 30, 1840

It is the nobility of their style which will make our writers of 1840 unreadable forty years from now.

Manuscript Note (1840)

LEIGH HUNT
(1784-1859)

Abou Ben Adhem (may his tribe increase!)
Awoke one night from a deep dream of peace.

Abou Ben Adhem (1838)

An angel writing in a book of gold.

Abou Ben Adhem (1838)

Write me as one who loves his fellowmen.

Abou Ben Adhem (1838)

And show'd the names whom love of God had bless'd,
And lo! Ben Adhem's name led all the rest.

Abou Ben Adhem (1838)

Stolen sweets are always sweeter,
Stolen kisses much completer,
Stolen looks are nice in chapels,
Stolen, stolen, be your apples.

Song of Fairies Robbing
an Orchard

The only place a new hat can be carried into with safety is a church, for there is plenty of room there.

A Chapter on Hats

The maid-servant, the sailor, and the schoolboy, are the three beings that enjoy a holiday beyond all the rest of the world.

The Maid-Servant

OLIVER HAZARD PERRY
(1785-1820)

We have met the enemy, and they are ours.

Letter to General Harrison (dated
"United States Brig Niagara. Off the
Western Sisters. Sept. 10, 1813, 4. P.M.")

JOHN PIERPONT
(1785-1866)

The Yankee boy, before he's sent to school,
Well knows the mystery of that magic tool,
The pocket-knife.

Whittling, a Yankee Portrait
Stanza 1

SAMUEL WOODWORTH
(1785-1842)

How dear to this heart are the scenes of my childhood,
When fond recollection presents them to view.

The Old Oaken Bucket

DAVID CROCKETT
(1786-1836)

I leave this rule for others when I'm dead,
Be always sure you're right—then go ahead.

Autobiography (1834)

WINFIELD SCOTT
(1786-1866)

Say to the seceded States, "Wayward sisters, depart in peace."

Letter to W.H. Seward
(March 3, 1861)

EMMA WILLARD
(1787-1870)

Rocked in the cradle of the deep,
I lay me down in peace to sleep.

The Cradle of the Deep (1831)

RICHARD HARRIS BARHAM
(1788-1845)

The Lady Jane was tall and slim,
The Lady Jane was fair.

Ingoldsby Legends (1840)
The Knight and the Lady

The Devil must be in that little Jackdaw!

Ingoldsby Legends
The Jackdaw of Rheims

The Cardinal rose with a dignified look,
He call'd for his candle, his bell, and his book!
In holy anger, and pious grief,
He solemnly cursed that rascally thief!
He cursed him at board, he cursed him in bed;
From the sole of his foot to the crown of his head;
He cursed him in sleeping, that every night
He should dream of the devil, and wake in a fright;
He cursed him in living, he cursed him in drinking,

He cursed him in coughing, in sneezing, in winking;
He cursed him in sitting, in standing, in lying;
He cursed him in walking, in riding, in flying,
He cursed him living, he cursed him dying!—
Never was heard such a terrible curse!
But what gave rise to no little surprise,
Nobody seem'd one penny the worse!

Ingoldsby Legends
The Jackdaw of Rheims

GEORGE NOEL GORDON, LORD BYRON
(1788-1824)

Near this spot are deposited the remains of one who possessed Beauty without Vanity, Strength without Insolence, Courage without Ferocity, and all the Virtues of Man, without his Vices. This Praise, which would be unmeaning Flattery if inscribed over human ashes, is but a just tribute to the Memory of Boatswain, a Dog.

Inscription on the Monument of
a Newfoundland Dog (1808)

I'll publish right or wrong:
Fools are my theme, let satire be my song.

English Bards and Scotch
Reviewers (1809), Line 5

With just enough of learning to misquote.

English Bards and Scotch
Reviewers (1809), Line 66

Maidens, like moths, are ever caught by glare,
And Mammon wins his way where seraphs might despair.

Childe Harold's Pilgrimage
Canto I (1812), Stanza 9

He who ascends to mountain-tops, shall find
The loftiest peaks most wrapt in clouds and snow;
He who surpasses or subdues mankind

Must look down on the hate of those below.

Childe Harold's Pilgrimage
Canto III, Stanza 45

Fame is the thirst of youth.

Childe Harold's Pilgrimage
Canto III, Stanza 112

I have not loved the world, nor the world me;
I have not flatter'd its rank breath, nor bow'd
To its idolatries a patient knee.

Childe Harold's Pilgrimage
Canto III, Stanza 113

The thorns which I have reap'd are of the tree
I planted; they have torn me, and I bleed.
I should have known what fruit would spring from such a seed.

Childe Harold's Pilgrimage
Canto IV, Stanza 10

"While stands the Coliseum, Rome shall stand;
When falls the Coliseum, Rome shall fall;
And when Rome falls—the world."

Childe Harold's Pilgrimage
Canto IV, Stanza 145

There is a pleasure in the pathless woods,
There is a rapture on the lonely shore,
There is society, where none intrudes,
By the deep sea, and music in its roar;
I love not man the less, but Nature more.

Childe Harold's Pilgrimage
Canto IV, Stanza 178

Roll on, thou deep and dark blue ocean, roll!
Ten thousand fleets sweep over thee in vain;
Man marks the earth with ruin—his control
Stops with the shore.

Childe Harold's Pilgrimage
Canto IV, Stanza 179

The Assyrian came down like the wolf on the fold,
And his cohorts were gleaming in purple and gold;
And the sheen of their spears was like stars on the sea,

When the blue wave rolls nightly on deep Galilee.

Hebrew Melodies (1815)
The Destruction of Sennacherib,
Stanza 1

Mont Blanc is the monarch of mountains;
They crowned him long ago
On a throne of rocks, in a robe of clouds,
With a diadem of snow.

Manfred (1817) Act I, Sc. 1

What men call gallantry, and gods adultery,
Is much more common where the climate's sultry.

Don Juan, Canto I
Stanza 63

A little still she strove, and much repented,
And whispering, "I will ne'er consent,"
—consented.

Don Juan, Canto I
Stanza 117

'Tis said that persons living on annuities
Are longer lived than others.

Don Juan, Canto II (1819)
Stanza 65

All who joy would win
Must share it—happiness was born a twin.

Don Juan, Canto II, Stanza 172

Let us have wine and women, mirth and laughter,
Sermons and soda-water the day after.

Don Juan, Canto II, Stanza 178

But words are things, and a small drop of ink,
Falling like dew upon a thought, produces
That which makes thousands, perhaps millions, think.

Don Juan, Canto III, Stanza 88

Death, so called, is a thing which makes men weep,
And yet a third of life is passed in sleep.

Don Juan, Canto XIV (1823)
Stanza 3

Of all the horrid, hideous notes of woe,

Sadder than owl-songs or the midnight blast,
Is that portentous phrase, "I told you so."

Don Juan, Canto XIV, Stanza 50

'Tis strange, but true; for truth is always strange—
Stranger than fiction.

Don Juan, Canto XIV, Stanza 101

The Devil hath not, in all his quiver's choice,
An arrow for the heart like a sweet voice.

Don Juan, Canto XV (1824)
Stanza 13

A lovely being, scarcely formed or moulded,
A rose with all its sweetest leaves yet folded.

Don Juan, Canto XV
Stanza 43

All farewells should be sudden.

Sardanapalus (1821), Act V

The world is a bundle of hay,
Mankind are the asses that pull,
Each tugs in a different way—
And the greatest of all is John Bull!

Letter to Thomas Moore (June 22, 1821)

He seems
To have seen better days, as who has not
Who has seen yesterday?

Werner (1822) Act I, Sc. 1

The 'good old times"—all times when old are good.

The Age of Bronze (1823)
Stanza 1

What's drinking?
A mere pause from thinking!

The Deformed Transformed
(1824) Act III, Sc. 1

ARTHUR SCHOPENHAUER
(1788-1860)

Hatred comes from the heart; contempt from the head; and

neither feeling is quite within our control.

Studies in Pessimism
Psychological Observations

If a man sets out to hate all the miserable creatures he meets, he will not have much energy left for anything else; whereas he can despise them, one and all, with the greatest ease.

Studies in Pessimism
Psychological Observations

Every man takes the limits of his own field of vision for the limits of the world.

Studies in Pessimism
Psychological Observations

The fundamental fault of the female character is that it has no sense of justice.

Studies in Pessimism
Psychological Observations

Do not shorten the morning by getting up late, look upon it as the quintessence of life, as to a certain extent sacred.

Counsels and Maxims, Chap. 2

HANNAH FLAGG GOULD
(1789-1865)

Alone I walked the ocean strand;
A pearly shell was in my hand;
I stooped and wrote upon the sand
My name—the year—the day.

A wave came rolling high and fast,
And washed my lines away.

A Name on the Sand, Stanza 1

WILLIAM KNOX
(1789-1825)

Oh why should the spirit of mortal be proud?
Like a fast-flitting meteor, a fast-flying cloud,
A flash of the lightning, a break of the wave,

He passes from life to his rest in the grave.

Songs of Israel (1824), Mortality
Stanza 1

'Tis the wink of an eye, 'tis the draught of a breath,
From the blossom of health to the paleness of death.

Songs of Israel (1824), Mortality
Stanza 14

SARAH JOSEPHA HALE
(1790-1879)

Mary had a little lamb,
  Its fleece was white as snow,
And everywhere that Mary went
  The lamb was sure to go;
He followed her to school one day,
  That was against the rule;
It made the children laugh and play
  To see a lamb in school.

Mary's Lamb. In the Juvenile
Miscellany (September, 1830)

JOHN HOWARD PAYNE
(1792-1852)

'Mid pleasures and palaces though we may roam,
Be it ever so humble, there's no place like home;
A charm from the skies seems to hallow us there,
Which sought through the world is ne'er met with elsewhere.

Home, Sweet Home (From the opera
Clari, the Maid of Milan, 1823)

PERCY BYSSHE SHELLEY
(1792-1822)

Once, early in the morning,
  Beelzebub arose,

With care his sweet person adorning,
  He put on his Sunday clothes.

> *The Devil's Walk, A Ballad*
> *(1812) Stanza 1*

How wonderful is Death,
Death and his brother Sleep.

> *Queen Mab (1813) I*

Power, like a desolating pestilence,
Pollutes whate'er it touches; and obedience,
Bane of all genius, virtue, freedom, truth,
Makes slaves of men, and, of the human frame,
A mechanized automaton.

> *Queen Mab (1813) III*

  All love is sweet,
Given or returned. Common as light is love,
And its familiar voice wearies not ever . . . .
They who inspire it most are fortunate,
As I am now; but those who feel it most
Are happier still.

> *Prometheus Unbound (1818-1819)*
> *Act II, Sc. 5*

  O Wind,
If Winter comes, can Spring be far behind?

> *Ode to the West Wind (1819)*
> *Stanza 5*

The seed ye sow, another reaps;
The wealth ye find, another keeps;
The robes ye weave, another wears;
The arms ye forge, another bears.

> *Song to the Men of England*
> *(1819) Stanza 5*

Nothing in the world is single,
All things by a law divine
In one spirit meet and mingle.

> *Love's Philosophy (1819)*
> *Stanza 1*

  Till the Future dares
Forget the Past, his fate and fame shall be

An echo and a light unto eternity!

Adonais, I

As long as skies are blue, and fields are green,
Evening must usher night, night urge the morrow,
Month follow month with woe, and year wake year to
  sorrow.

Adonais, XXI

The flower that smiles today
  Tomorrow dies;
All that we wish to stay
  Tempts and then flies.
What is this world's delight?
Lightning that mocks the night.
  Brief even as bright.

Mutability (1821) II, Stanza 1

  When the lamp is shattered
The light in the dust lies dead:—
  When the cloud is scattered
The rainbow's glory is shed.

When the Lamp Is Shattered (1822)
Stanza 1

Sing again, with your dear voice revealing
  A tone
 Of some world far from ours,
Where music and moonlight and feeling
  Are one.

To Jane: The Keen Stars Were
Twinkling (1822) Stanza 4

JOHN CLARE
(1793-1864)

I am! yet what I am who cares, or knows?
My friends forsake me like a memory lost.

Written in Northampton County Asylum

The world was on thy page
Of victories but a comma.

To Napoleon

If life had a second edition, how I would correct the proofs.
In a letter to a friend. Quoted in
Foreword to J.W. and Anne Tibble's
John Clare: A Life (1932)

FELICIA DOROTHEA HEMANS
(1793-1835)

The boy stood on the burning deck,
  Whence all but he had fled;
The flame that lit the battle's wreck
  Shone round him o'er the dead.

Casabianca, Stanza 1

There came a burst of thunder sound;
The boy—oh! where was he.

Casabianca, Stanza 9

WILLIAM CULLEN BRYANT
(1794-1878)

To him who in the love of Nature holds
Communion with her visible forms, she speaks
A various language.

Thanatopsis (1817-1821)

    All that tread
The globe are but a handful to the tribes
That slumber in its bosom.

Thanatopsis (1817-1821)

So live, that when thy summons comes to join
The innumerable caravan which moves
To that mysterious realm, where each shall take
His chamber in the silent halls of death,
Thou go not, like the quarry-slave at night,
Scourged to his dungeon, but, sustained and soothed
By an unfaltering trust, approach thy grave,
Like one that wraps the drapery of his couch
About him, and lies down to pleasant dreams.

Thanatopsis (1817-1821)

Truth, crushed to earth, shall rise again.
  The eternal years of God are hers;
But Error, wounded, writhes in pain,
  And dies among his worshippers.

The Battle-Field, Stanza 9

  Man foretells afar
The courses of the stars; the very hour
He knows when they shall darken or grow bright;
Yet doth the eclipse of Sorrow and of Death
Come unforewarned.

An Evening Revery

EDWARD EVERETT
(1794-1865)

As a work of art, I know few things more pleasing to the eye, or more capable of affording scope and gratification to a taste for the beautiful, than a well-situated, well-cultivated farm.

Address at Buffalo, New York
(October 9, 1857)

I am no aristocrat. I do not own a quadruped larger than a cat, and she an indifferent mouser; nor any kind of vehicle, with the exception, possibly, of a wheelbarrow.

Mount Vernon Papers, No. 7

JOHN GARDINER CALKINS BRAINARD
(1795-1828)

Death has shaken out the sands of thy glass.

Lament for Long Tom

NARCISSE ACHILLE,
COMTE DE SALVANDY
(1795-1856)

We are dancing on a volcano.

At a fete given by the Duc d'Orleans
to the King of Naples (1830)

THOMAS CARLYLE
(1795-1881)

He who would write heroic poems should make his whole life a heroic poem.
> *Life of Schiller (1823-1824)*

The great law of culture is: Let each become all that he was created capable of being.
> *Richter (1827)*

In every man's writings, the character of the writer must lie recorded.
> *Goethe (1828)*

Aesop's Fly, sitting on the axle of the chariot, has been much laughed at for exclaiming: What a dust I do raise!
> *On Boswell's Life of Johnson (1832)*

Whoso belongs only to his own age, and reverences only its gilt Popinjays or soot-smeared Mumbojumbos, must needs die with it.
> *On Boswell's Life of Johnson (1832)*

Love is ever the beginning of Knowledge, as fire is of light.
> *Essays. Death of Goethe (1832)*

Music is well said to be the speech of angels.
> *Essays. The Opera*

Be not the slave of Words.
> *Sartor Resartus (1833-1834)*
> *Book I, Chap. 8*

Wonder is the basis of Worship.
> *Sartor Resartus (1833-1834)*
> *Book I, Chap. 10*

Biography is by nature the most universally profitable, universally pleasant of all things; especially biography of distinguished individuals.
> *Sartor Resartus (1833-1834)*
> *Book I, Chap. 11*

What you see, yet cannot see over, is as good as infinite.
> *Sartor Resartus (1833-1834)*
> *Book II, Chap. 1*

As the Swiss inscription says: Sprechen ist silbern, Schweigen ist golden—"Speech is silvern, Silence is golden"; or, as I might rather express it, Speech is of Time, Silence is of Eternity.

Sartor Resartus, Book III, Chap. 3

Wouldst thou plant for Eternity, then plant into the deep infinite faculties of man.

Sartor Resartus, Book III, Chap. 3

Two men I honour, and no third. First the toilworn craftsman that with earth-made implement laboriously conquers the earth, and makes her man's . . . . A second man I honour, and still more highly: Him who is seen toiling for the spiritually indispensable; not daily bread but the bread of life.

Sartor Resartus, Book III, Chap. 4

That there should one man die ignorant who had capacity for knowledge, this I call a tragedy.

Sartor Resartus, Book III, Chap. 4

No man lives without jostling and being jostled; in all ways he has to elbow himself through the world, giving and receiving offence.

Sir Walter Scott (1838)

All greatness is unconscious, or it is little and naught.

Sir Walter Scott (1838)

Democracy is, by the nature of it, a self-cancelling business; and gives in the long run a net result of zero.

Chartism (1839) Chap. 6,
Laissez-Faire

The history of the world is but the biography of great men.

Heroes and Hero-Worship
The Hero as Divinity

"A fair day's wages for a fair day's work"; it is as just a demand as governed men ever made of governing. It is the everlasting right of man.

Past and Present (1843)
Book I, Chap. 3

Every noble crown is, and on earth will forever be, a crown of thorns.

Past and Present, Book III, Chap. 4

Even in the meanest sorts of Labor, the whole soul of a man is composed into a kind of real harmony the instant he sets himself to work.

Past and Present, Book III, Chap. 11

So here hath been dawning
   Another blue day:
Think, wilt thou let it
   Slip useless away?

Today

What is Man? A foolish baby,
   Vainly strives, and fights, and frets.
Demanding all, deserving nothing,
   One small grave is what he gets.

Cui Bono, Stanza 3

JOSEPH RODMAN DRAKE
(1795-1820)

When Freedom from her mountain height
   Unfurled her standard to the air,
She tore the azure robe of night,
   And set the stars of glory there.
She mingled with its gorgeous dyes
The milky baldric of the skies,
And striped its pure, celestial white
With streakings of the morning light.

The American Flag (1819), Stanza 1

Forever float that standard sheet!
   Where breathes the foe but falls before us,
With Freedom's soil beneath our feet,
   And Freedom's banner streaming oe'r us?

The American Flag (1819), Stanza 5

JOHN KEATS
(1795-1821)

To one who has been long in city pent,
'Tis very sweet to look into the fair

And open face of heaven.

Sonnet, To One Who Has
Been Long in City Pent

The poetry of earth is never dead.

On the Grasshopper
and the Cricket

    Life is but a day;
A fragile dew-drop on its perilous way
From a tree's summit.

Sleep and Poetry, Line 85

Shed no tear—O shed no tear!
The flower will bloom another year.
Weep no more—O weep no more!
Young buds sleep in the root's white core.

Faery Songs. I (Written 1818)

Blue! Gentle cousin of the forest-green,
Married to green in all the sweetest flowers—
Forget-me-not—the blue bell—and, that Queen
Of secrecy, the violet.

Sonnet, Blue (Written 1818)

A thing of beauty is a joy for ever:
Its loveliness increases; it will never
Pass into nothingness; but still will keep
A bower quiet for us, and a sleep
Full of sweet dreams, and health, and quiet breathing.

Endymion (1818) Book I, Line 1

    To sorrow,
    I bade good-morrow,
And thought to leave her far away behind;
    But cheerly, cheerly,
    She loves me dearly;
She is so constant to me, and so kind.

Endymion, Book IV, Line 173

Pillow'd upon my fair love's ripening breast,
To feel for ever its soft fall and swell,
Awake for ever in a sweet unrest,
Still, still to hear her tender-taken breath,

And so live ever—or else swoon to death.
                    Sonnet, Bright Star (Written 1819)

The day is gone, and all its sweets are gone!
Sweet voice, sweet lips, soft hand, and softer breast.
                    Sonnet, The Day Is Gone (Written 1819)

Was it a vision, or a waking dream?
Fled is that music:—Do I wake or sleep?
                    Ode to a Nightingale,
                                    Stanza 8

Heard melodies are sweet, but those unheard
Are sweeter.
                    Ode on a Grecian Urn
                                    Stanza 2

"Beauty is truth, truth beauty,"—that is all
Ye know on earth, and all ye need to know.
                    Ode on a Grecian Urn
                                    Stanza 5

    For to bear all naked ʾruths,
And to envisage circumstance, all calm,
That is the top of sovereignty.
                    Hyperion, Book II, Line 203

HARTLEY COLERIDGE
(1796-1849)

The soul of man is larger than the sky,
Deeper than ocean, or the abysmal dark
Of the unfathomed center.

                    To Shakespeare

She is not fair to outward view
    As many maidens be;
Her loveliness I never knew
    Until she smiled on me:
Oh! then I saw her eye was bright,
A well of love, a spring of light.

                    Song, She Is Not Fair

Her very frowns are fairer far
Than smiles of other maidens are.

Song, She Is Not Fair

HORACE MANN
(1796-1859)

Lost, yesterday, somewhere between sunrise and sunset, two golden hours, each set with sixty diamond minutes. No reward is offered, for they are gone forever.

Aphorism

Be ashamed to die until you have won some victory for humanity.

Commencement Address,
Antioch College (1859)

THOMAS HAYNES BAYLY
(1797-1839)

Those who have wealth must be watchful and wary,
Power, alas! naught but misery brings!

I'd Be a Butterfly, Stanza 2

Why don't the men propose, Mamma?
Why don't the men propose?

Why Don't the Men Propose?

Absence makes the heart grow fonder:
Isle of Beauty, fare thee well!

Isle of Beauty

HEINRICH HEINE
(1797-1856)

"Oh, 'tis Love that makes us grateful,
Oh, 'tis Love that makes us rich!"
So sings man, and every fateful
Echo bears his amorous speech.

O, die Liebe macht uns selig,
Stanza 1

A pine tree stands so lonely
In the North where the high winds blow,
He sleeps; and the whitest blanket
Wraps him in ice and snow.

Ein Fichtenbaum steht einsam,
Stanza 1

The years keep coming and going,
  Men will arise and depart;
Only one thing is immortal:
  The love that is in my heart.

Die Jahre kommen und gehen,
Stanza 1

This is America!
This is the new world!
Not the present European
Wasted and withering sphere.

Vitzliputzli. Prelude, Dieses ist
Amerika! Stanza 1

For Sleep is good, but Death is better still—
The best is never to be born at all.

Gross ist die Ahnlichkeit der
beiden schonen

If one has no heart, one cannot write for the masses.

Letter to Julius Campe
(March 18, 1840)

WILLIAM MOTHERWELL
(1797-1835)

I've wandered east, I've wandered west,
  Through mony a weary way;
But never, never can forget
  The luve o' life's young day!

Jeannie Morrison, Stanza 1

ROBERT GILFILLAN
(1798-1850)

There's a hope for every woe,

And a balm for every pain,
But the first joys of our heart
Come never back again!

The Exile's Song. Stanza 4

THOMAS HOOD
(1798-1845)

Ben Battle was a soldier bold,
And used to war's alarms;
But a cannon-ball took off his legs.
So he laid down his arms!

Faithless Nellie Gray (1826)
Stanza I

I remember, I remember
The house where I was born,
The little window where the sun
Came peeping in at morn;
He never came a wink too soon
Nor brought too long a day.

I Remember, I Remember
(1827) Stanza I

And there is even a happiness
That makes the heart afraid.

Ode to Melancholy (1827)

There's not a string attuned to mirth
But has its chord in melancholy.

Ode to Melancholy (1827)

Peace and rest at length have come,
All the day's long toil is past,
And each heart is whispering, "Home,
Home at last."

Home at Last (1827)

O bed! O bed! delicious bed!
That heaven upon earth to the weary head!

Miss Kilmansegg and Her Precious Leg
(1841-1843) Her Dream, Stanza 7

He lies like a hedgehog rolled up the wrong way,
Tormenting himself with his prickles.

Miss Kilmansegg and Her Precious Leg
(1841-1843) Her Dream, Stanza 14

O God! that bread should be so dear,
And flesh and blood so cheap!

The Song of the Shirt (1843)
Stanza 5

ROBERT POLLOK
(1798-1827)

Sorrows remembered sweeten present joy.

The Course of Time. Book I, Line 464

HONORE DE BALZAC
(1799-1850)

I believe in the incomprehensibility of God.

Letter to Madame de Hanska (1837)

Those sweetly smiling angels with pensive looks, innocent
faces, and cash-boxes for hearts.

Cousin Bette (1846) Chap. 15

Love and hate are emotions that feed on themselves; but of the
two hate is the more enduring. Love is limited by our limited
strength—it draws its power from living and giving; but hate is
like death and avarice—it is a sort of active abstraction, apart
from people and things.

Cousin Bette (1846) Chap. 16

GEORGE PAYNE
RAINSFORD JAMES
(1799-1860)

Thou'rt an ass, Robin, thou'rt an ass,
To think that great men be
More gay than I that lie on the grass
Under the greenwood tree.

I tell thee no, I tell thee no,
The Great are slaves to their gilded show.

Richelieu (1829) Chap. 3,
Robber's Song, Stanza I

Turning over a page or two in the book of Nature, I found that the most brilliant actions and the greatest events were generally brought about from the meanest motives and most petty causes.

Richelieu (1829) Chap. 5

THOMAS BABINGTON LORD MACAULAY
(1800-1859)

The English Bible,—a book which if everything else in our language should perish, would alone suffice to show the whole extent of its beauty and power.

On John Dryden (1828)

His imagination resembled the wings of an ostrich. It enabled him to run, though not to soar.

On John Dryden (1828)

Men are never so likely to settle a question rightly as when they discuss it freely.

Southey's Colloquies (1820)

From the poetry of Lord Byron they drew a system of ethics compounded of misanthropy and voluptuousness,—a system in which the two great commandments were to hate your neighbour and to love your neighbour's wife.

On Moore's Life of Lord Byron

The conformation of his mind was such that whatever was little seemed to him great, and whatever was great seemed to him little.

On Horace Walpole (1833)

The highest proof of virtue is to possess boundless power without abusing it.

Review of Aikin's Life of
Addison (1843)

There were gentlemen and there were seamen in the navy of Charles II. But the seamen were not gentlemen, and the gentlemen were not seamen.

History of England (1849-1861)
Vol. Chap. 3

Soon fades the spell, soon comes the night;
Say will it not be then the same,
Whether we played the black or white,
Whether we lost or won the game?

Sermon in a Churchyard. Stanza 8

Who never forgot that the end of Government is the happiness of the governed.

Inscription for the Statue of
Lord William Bentinck

SIR HENRY TAYLOR
(1800-1886)

His food
Was glory, which was poison to his mind
And peril to his body.

Philip Van Artevelde (1834).
Park I, Act I, Sc. 5

He that lacks time to mourn, lacks time to mend. Eternity mourns that.

Philip Van Artevelde (1834)
Part I, Act I, Sc. 5

JANE WELSH CARLYLE
(1801-1866)

Never does one feel oneself so utterly helpless as in trying to speak comfort for great bereavement. I will not try it. Time is the only comforter for the loss of a mother.

Letter to Thomas Carlyle
(December 27, 1853)

When one has been threatened with a great injustice, one accepts a smaller as a favour.

Journal, November 21, 1855

JOHN HENRY, CARDINAL NEWMAN
(1801-1890)

Time hath a taming hand.

Persecution (1832). Stanza 3

Growth is the only evidence of life.

Apologia pro Vita Sua (1864)

BRIGHAM YOUNG
(1801-1877)

This is the place!

*On first seeing the valley of the
Great Salt Lake, July 24, 1847*

ALLEN C. SPOONER
(Floruit 1846)

I mused upon the Pilgrim flock
Whose luck it was to land
Upon almost the only rock
Among the Plymouth sand.

*Old Times and New. Stanza 2
(Written for the New England
Society Festival, New York.
December 22, 1846)*

ALEXANDRE DUMAS
THE ELDER
(1802-1870)

There are virtues which become crimes by exaggeration.

*The Count of Monte Cristo
(1841-1845). Chap. 90*

Great is truth. Fire cannot burn, nor water drown it.

*The Count of Monte Cristo
(1841-1845) Chap. 113*

All human wisdom is summed up in two words,—wait and hope.

> The Count of Monte Cristo
> (1841-1845) Chap. 117

All for one, one for all, that is our device.

> The Three Musketeers (1844)
> Chap. 9

Nothing succeeds like success.

> Ange Pitou (1854). Vol. I, Page 72

Let us look for the woman.

> The Mohicans of Paris
> (1854-1855). Vol. III, Chaps. 10 & 11

VICTOR HUGO
(1802-1885)

Let us, while waiting for new monuments, preserve the ancient monuments.

> Note added to the Definitive Edition
> of Notre Dame de Paris (1832)

Great blunders are often made, like large ropes, of a multitude of fibres.

> Les Miserables (1862)
> Cosette, Book V, Chap. 10

Upon the first goblet he read this inscription: Monkey wine; upon the second: lion wine; upon the third: sheep wine; upon the fourth: swine wine. These four inscriptions expressed the four descending degrees of drunkenness: the first, that which enlivens; the second, that which irritates; the third, that which stupefies; finally the last, that which brutalizes.

> Les Miserables (1862)
> Cosette, Book VI, Chap. 9

A man is not idle because he is absorbed in thought. There is a visible labour and there is an invisible labour.

> Les Miserables. Cosette,
> Book VII, Chap. 8

A creditor is worse than a master; for a master owns only your person, a creditor owns your dignity, and can belabour that.

Les Miserables. Marius
Book V, Chap. 2

Where the telescope ends, the microscope begins. Which of the two has the grander view?

Les Miserables. Saint Denis,
Book III, Chap. 3

A compliment is something like a kiss through a veil.

Les Miserables, Saint Denis
Book VIII, Chap. I

Philosophy is the microscope of thought.

Les Miserables. Jean Valjean
Book II, Chap. 2

When grace is joined with wrinkles, it is adorable. There is an unspeakable dawn in happy old age.

Les Miserables. Jean Valjean
Book V, Chap. 2

Nothing is so like a soul as a bee. It goes from flower to flower as a soul from star to star, and it gathers honey as a soul gathers light.

Ninety-Three (1879), Part III
Book III, Chap. 3

LYDIA MARIA CHILD
(1802-1880)

Over the river and through the wood,
To grandfather's house we'll go;
The horse knows the way
To carry the sleigh,
Through the white and drifted snow.

Thanksgiving Day. Stanza 1

EDWARD COOTE PINKNEY
(1802-1828)

Look out upon the stars, my love,
And shame them with thine eyes.

A Serenade (1825)

WINTHROP MACKWORTH PRAED
(1802-1839)

Dame Fortune is a fickle gipsy,
And always blind, and often tipsy;
Sometimes for years and years together,
She'll bless you with the sunniest weather,
Bestowing honour, pudding, pence,
You can't imagine why or whence;—
Then in a moment—Presto, pass!—
Your joys are withered like the grass.

The Haunted Tree

THOMAS LOVELL BEDDOES
(1803-1849)

The anchor heaves, the ship swings free,
The sails swell full. To sea, to sea!

Sailor's Song. Stanza 2

If there were dreams to sell,
What would you buy?
Some cost a passing-bell;
Some a light sigh.

Dream-Pedlary

That divinest hope, which none can know of
Who have not laid their dearest in the grave.

Death's Jest Book (1850)

If thou wilt ease thine heart
Of love and all its smart,
Then sleep, dear, sleep.
But wilt thou cure thy heart
Of love and all its smart,
Then die, dear, die.

Death's Jest Book (1850)

WILLIAM ALLEN
(1803-1879)

Fifty-four forty, or fight!

Speech, U.S. Senate (1844)

RALPH WALDO EMERSON
(1803-1882)

Wherever Macdonald sits, there is the head of the table.

The American Scholar (1837)

Men grind and grind in the mill of a truism, and nothing comes out but what was put in. But the moment they desert the tradition for a spontaneous thought, then poetry, wit, hope, virtue, learning, anecdote, all flock to their aid.

Literary Ethics (1838)

Whoso would be a man must be a non-conformist.

Essays: First Series (1841)
Self-Reliance

To be great is to be misunderstood.

Essays: First Series (1841)
Self-Reliance

An institution is the lengthened shadow of one man.

Essays: First Series (1841)
Self-Reliance

Nothing can bring you peace but yourself.

Essays: First Series (1841)
Self-Reliance

Every sweet has its sour; every evil its good.

Essays: First Series (1841)
Self-Reliance

For every thing you have missed, you have gained something else; and for every thing you gain, you lose something.

Essays: First Series (1841)
Self-Reliance

All mankind love a lover.

Essays: First Series. Love

A friend is a person with whom I may be sincere. Before him, I may think aloud.

Essays: First Series. Friendship

The only reward of virtue is virtue; the only way to have a friend is to be one.

Essays: First Series. Friendship

The reward of a thing well done, is to have done it.

Essays: Second Series (1844)
New England Reformers

Life is too short to waste
In critic peep or cynic bark,
Quarrel or reprimand:
'Twill soon be dark;
Up! mind thine own aim, and
God speed the mark!

Poems. To J. W.

If eyes were made for seeing,
Then Beauty is its own excuse for being.

Poems. The Rhodora

When nature removes a great man, people explore the horizon for a successor; but none comes, and none will. His class is extinguished with him. In some other and quite different field, the next man will appear.

Representative Men (1850)
Uses of Great Men

Every hero becomes a bore at last.

Represenative Men (1850)
Uses of Great Men

Great geniuses have the shortest biographies.

Representative Men (1850)
Plato, or, The Philosopher

Keep cool: it will be all one a hundred years hence.

Representative Men (1850)
Montaigne, or, The Skeptic

Is not marriage an open question, when it is alleged, from the beginning of the world, that such as are in the institution wish to get out, and such as are out wish to get in?

Representative Men
Montaigne, or, The Skeptic

Art is a jealous mistress, and, if a man have a genius for painting, poetry, music, architecture, or philosophy, he makes a bad husband, and an ill-provider.

Conduct of Life (1860) Wealth

The highest compact we can make with our fellow is,—"Let
there be truth between us two forevermore."
Conduct of Life (1860) Behavior

Beauty without grace is the hook without the bait.
Conduct of Life
Considerations by the Way

The music that can deepest reach,
And cure all ill, is cordial speech.
May-Day and Other Pieces
Merlin's Song

Hitch your wagon to a star.
Society and Solitude (1870)
Civilization

Can anybody remember when the times were not hard and
money not scarce?
Society and Solitude (1870)
Works and Days

Life is not so short but that there is always time enough for
courtesy.
Letters and Social Aims (1876)
Social Aims

Wit makes its own welcome, and levels all distinctions.
Letters and Social Aims
The Comic

The perception of the comic is a tie of sympathy with other
men.
Letters and Social Aims
The Comic

What is a weed? A plant whose virtues havs not yet been dis-
covered.
Fortune of the Republic (1878)

RICHARD HENRY HENGIST HORNE
(1803-1884)

Tis always morning somewhere in the world.
Orion (1843) Book III, Canto II

DOUGLAS JERROLD
(1803-1857)

He is one of those wise philanthropists who in a time of famine would vote for nothing but a supply of toothpicks.

Wit and Opinions of Douglas
Jerrold (1859)

Some people are so fond of ill-luck that they run half-way to meet it.

Wit and Opinions of Douglas Jerrold
Meeting Troubles Half-Way

Talk to him of Jacob's ladder, and he would ask the number of the steps.

Wit and Opinions of Douglas Jerrold
A Matter-of-fact Man

CHARLES SWAIN
(1803-1874)

Let tomorrow take care of tomorrow,—
Leave things of the future to fate;
What's the use to anticipate sorrow?—
Life's troubles come never too late!

Imaginary Evils. Stanza I

EDWARD BULWER LYTTON
(1803-1873)

A good heart is better than all the heads in the world.

The Disowned (1828) Chap. 33

The easiest person to deceive is one's own self.

The Disowned (1828) Chap. 42

The magic of the tongue is the most dangerous of all spells.

Eugene Aram (1832) Book I, Chap. 7

Love, like Death,
Levels all ranks, and lays the shepherd's crook
Beside the sceptre.

The Lady of Lyons (1838)
Act III, Sc. 2

In the Lexicon of youth, which fate reserves
For a bright manhood, there is no such word
As "fail."

Richelieu, Act. II, Sc. 2

BENJAMIN DISRAELI,
EARL OF BEACONSFIELD
(1804-1881)

Experience is the child of Thought, and Thought is the child of Action. We can not learn men from books.

Vivian Grey (1826)
Book V, Chap. I

Variety is the mother of Enjoyment.

Vivian Grey (1826)
Book V, Chap. IV

I repeat . . . that all power is a trust; that we are accountable for its exercise; that from the people and for the people all springs, and all must exist.

Vivian Grey (1826)
Book VI, Chap. VII

Man is not the creature of circumstances. Circumstances are the creatures of men.

Vivian Grey (1826)
Book VI, Chap. VII

Yes, I am a Jew, and when the ancestors of the right honourable gentleman were brutal savages in an unknown island, mine were priests in the temple of Solomon.

Reply to a taunt by
Daniel O'Connell

Though I sit down now, the time will come when you will hear me.

Maiden Speech in the House of
Commons (1837)

Youth is a blunder; manhood a struggle; old age a regret.

Coningsby (1844) Book III, Chap. I

Property has its duties as well as its rights.

Sybil (1845) Book II, Chap. XI

Little things affect little minds.
> *Sybil (1845) Book III, Chap. II*

We all of us live too much in a circle.
> *Sybil (1845) Book III, Chap. VII*

Everything comes if a man will only wait.
> *Tancred (1847) Book IV, Chap. VIII*

A precedent embalms a principle.
> *Speech on the Expenditures of the*
> *Country (February 22, 1848)*

Is man an ape or an angel? I, my lord, I am on the side of the angels. I repudiate with indignation and abhorrence those new fangled theories.
> *Speech at Oxford Diocesan*
> *Conference (November 25, 1864)*

Every woman should marry—and no man.
> *Lothair, Chap. XXX*

You know who the critics are? The men who have failed in literature and art.
> *Lothair, Chap. XXXV*

The hare-brained chatter of irresponsible frivolity.
> *Speech, Guildhall, London*
> *(November 9, 1878)*

His Christianity was muscular.
> *Endymion (1880) Chap. XIV*

NATHANIEL HAWTHORNE
(1804-1864)

Sleeping or waking, we hear not the airy footsteps of the strange things that almost happen.
> *Twice-Told Tales (1837)*
> *David Swan*

The sky, now gloomy as an author's prospects.
> *Twice-Told Tales (1837)*
> *Sights from a Steeple*

Human nature will not flourish, any more than a potato, if it be planted and replanted, for too long a series of generations, in the same worn-out soil.

The Scarlet Letter (1850)
The Custom-House

The black flower of civilized society, a prison.

The Scarlet Letter
Chapter 1

On the breast of her gown, in red cloth, surrounded with an elaborate embroidery and fantastic flourishes of gold-thread, appeared the letter A.

The Scarlet Letter
Chap. 2

No man, for any considerable period, can wear one face to himself, and another to the multitude, without finally getting bewildered as to which may be the true.

The Scarlet Letter
Chap. 20

Life is made up of marble and mud.

The House of the Seven Gables
(1851) Chap. 2

What other dungeon is so dark as one's own heart! What jailer so inexorable as one's self!

The House of the Seven Gables
(1851) Chap. 11

Once in every half-century, at longest, a family should be merged into the great, obscure mass of humanity, and forget all about its ancestors.

The House of the Seven Gables
Chap. 12

ALEXIS DE TOCQUEVILLE
(1805-1859)

I know of no country, indeed, where the love of money has taken stronger hold on the affections of men and where a profounder contempt is expressed for the theory of the permanent equality of property.

Democracy in America. Part I
(1835), Chap. 3

An American cannot converse, but he can discuss, and his talk falls into a dissertation. He speaks to you as if he was addressing a meeting; and if he should chance to become warm in the discussion, he will say "Gentlemen" to the person with whom he is conversing.

Democracy in America. Part I
Chap. 14

America is a land of wonders, in which everything is in constant motion and every change seems an improvement. The idea of novelty is there indissolubly connected with the idea of amelioration. No natural boundary seems to be set to the efforts of man; and in his eyes what is not yet done is only what he had not yet attempted to do.

Democracy in America, Part I
Chap. 18

WILLIAM LLOYD GARRISON
(1805-1879)

My Country is the world; my countrymen are mankind.

Prospectus of The Public Liberator
(1830)

I am in earnest. I will not equivocate; I will not excuse; I will not retreat a single inch; and I will be heard!

Salutatory of the Liberator
(January 1, 1831)

I will be as harsh as truth and as uncompromising as justice.

The Liberator. Vol. I, No. I
(1831)

With reasonable men, I will reason; with humane men I will plead; but to tyrants I will give no quarter, nor waste arguments where they will certainly be lost.

W.P. and F.J.T. Garrison:
William Lloyd Garrison (1885-1889)
Vol. I, Page 188

You can not possibly have a broader basis for any government than that which includes all the people, with all their rights in their hands, and with an equal power to maintain their rights.

W.P. and F.J.T. Garrison:
William Lloyd Garrison
Vol. IV, Page 224

WILLIAM PITT PALMER
(1805-1884)

I couldn't stand it, sir, at all,
But up and kissed her on the spot!
I know—boo-hoo—I ought to not,
But, somehow, from her looks—boo-hoo—
I thought she kind o'wished me to!

The Smack in School

COLONEL SIDNEY SHERMAN
(1805-1873)

Remember the Alamo!

Battle Cry, San Jacinto
(April 21, 1836)

JOHN STUART MILL
(1806-1873)

The sole end for which mankind are warranted, individually or collectively, in interfering with the liberty of action of any of their number is self-protection.

Liberty (1859) Introduction

If all mankind minus one, were of one opinion, and only one person were of the contrary opinion, mankind would be no more justified in silencing that one person, than he, if he had the power, would be justified in silencing mankind.

Liberty (1859) Chap. 2

We can never be sure that the opinion we are endeavoring to stifle is a false opinion; and if we were sure, stifling it would be an evil still.

Liberty (1859) Chap. 2

ELIZABETH BARRETT BROWNING
(1806-1861)

Of all the thoughts of God that are
Borne inward into souls afar,
Along the Psalmist's music deep,
Now tell me if that any is,
For gift or grace, surpassing this:
"He giveth his beloved—sleep."

The Sleep (1838) Stanza I

"Yes," I answered you last night;
"No," this morning, sir, I say:
Colors seen by candle-light
Will not look the same by day.

The Lady's "Yes" (1844) Stanza I

The beautiful seems right
By force of Beauty, and the feeble wrong
Because of weakness.

Aurora Leigh (1857), Book I, Line 753

God answers sharp and sudden on some prayers,
And thrusts the thing we have prayed for in our face,
A gauntlet with a gift in 't.

Aurora Leigh, Book II, Line 952

How many desolate creatures on the earth
Have learnt the simple dues of fellowship
And social comfort, in a hospital.

Aurora Leigh, Book III, Line 1122

A little sunburnt by the glare of life.

Aurora Leigh, Book IV, Line 1140

Let no one till his death
Be called unhappy. Measure not the work
Until the day's out and the labor done.

Aurora Leigh, Book V, Line 76

Earth's crammed with heaven,
And every common bush afire with God;
But only he who sees takes off his shoes—
The rest sit round it and pluck blackberries.

Aurora Leigh, Book VII, Line 820

HENRY WADSWORTH LONGFELLOW
(1807-1882)

Music is the universal language of mankind,—poetry their
universal pastime and delight.

Outre-Mer (1833-1834)

Tell me not, in mournful numbers,
Life is but an empty dream!
For the soul is dead that slumbers,
And things are not what they seem.

A Psalm of Life (1839) Stanza I

Life is real! Life is earnest!
And the grave is not its goal;
Dust thou art, to dust returnest,
Was not spoken of the soul.

A Psalm of Life (1839) Stanza I

Lives of great men all remind us
We can make our lives sublime,
And, departing, leave behind us
Footprints on the sands of time.

A Psalm of Life (1839) Stanza 7

Look not mournfully into the Past. It comes not back again.
Wisely improve the Present. It is thine. Go forth to meet the
shadowy Future, without fear, and with a manly heart.

Hyperion. Book IV, Chap. 8

Under the spreading chestnut-tree
The village smithy stands;
The smith a mighty man is he
With large and sinewy hands.

The Village Blacksmith (1842)
Stanza I

His brow is wet with honest sweat,
He earns whate'er he can,
And looks the whole world in the face,
For he owes not any man.

The Village Blacksmith (1842)
Stanza 2

Into each life some rain must fall,
Some days must be dark and dreary.
The Rainy Day (1842) Stanza 3

Were half the power, that fills the world with terror,
Were half the wealth, bestowed on camps and courts,
Given to redeem the human mind from error,
There were no need for arsenals or forts.
The Arsenal at Springfield
(1845) Stanza 9

The day is done, and the darkness
Falls from the wings of Night,
As a feather is wafted downward
From an eagle in his flight.
The Day Is Done (1845)
Stanza I

And the night shall be filled with music,
And the cares, that infest the day,
Shall fold their tents, like the Arabs,
And as silently steal away.
The Day Is Done, Stanza 11

I shot an arrow into the air,
It fell to earth, I knew not where.
The Arrow and the Song
(1845) Stanza 1

Though the mills of God grind slowly,
yet they grind exceeding small;
Though with patience He stands waiting, with exactness
grinds He all.
Retribution

This is the forest primeval. The murmuring pines and the
hemlocks.
Evangeline (1847) Prelude

Sail on, O Ship of State!
Sail on, O Union, strong and great!
Humanity with all its fears,
With all the hopes of future years,
Is hanging breathless on thy fate!
The Building of the Ship (1849)

By the shore of Gitche Gumee,
By the shining Big-Sea-Water,
Stood the wigwam of Nokomis,
Daughter of the Moon, Nokomis.

The Song of Hiawatha (1855) Part III

As unto the bow the cord is,
So unto the man is woman,
Though she bends him, she obeys him,
Though she draws him, yet she follows,
Useless each without the other!

The Song of Hiawatha (1855) Part X

"Why don't you speak for yourself, John?"

*The Courtship of Miles Standish
(1858) Part III*

The long mysterious Exodus of death.

*The Jewish Cemetery at Newport
(1858) Stanza I*

Pride and humiliation hand in hand
Walked with them through the world where'er they went;
Trampled and beaten were they as the sand,
And yet unshaken as the continent.

*The Jewish Cemetery at Newport
(1858) Stanza 12*

Between the dark and the daylight,
When the night is beginning to lower,
Comes a pause in the day's occupations,
That is known as the Children's Hour.

*The Children's Hour (1860)
Stanza I*

Listen, my children, and you shall hear,
Of the midnight ride of Paul Revere,
On the eighteenth of April, in Seventy-five;
Hardly a man is now alive
Who remembers that famous day and year.

*Tales of a Wayside Inn (1863-1874)
Paul Revere's Ride, Stanza I*

One if by land, and two if by sea;

And I on the opposite shore will be,
Ready to ride and spread the alarm
Through every Middlesex village and farm.
Tales of a Wayside Inn (1863-1874)
Paul Revere's Ride, Stanza 2

The fate of a nation was riding that night.
Tales of a Wayside Inn (1863-1874)
Paul Revere's Ride, Stanza 8

A voice in the darkness, a knock at the door,
And a word that shall echo forevermore!
Tales of a Wayside Inn (1863-1874)
Paul Revere's Ride, Stanza 14

A town that boasts inhabitants like me
Can have no lack of good society.
Tales of a Wayside Inn (1863-1874)
The Birds of Killingworth, Stanza 6

Ships that pass in the night, and speak each other in passing,
Only a signal shown and a distant voice in the darkness;
So on the ocean of life we pass and speak one another,
Only a look and a voice; then darkness again and a silence.
Tales of a Wayside Inn
Elizabeth IV

Time has laid his hand
Upon my heart, gently, not smiting it,
But as a harper lays his open palm
Upon his harp to deaden its vibrations.
The Golden Legend (1872) IV
The Cloisters

Don't cross the bridge till you come to it,
Is a proverb old, and of excellent wit.
The Golden Legend (1872) VI
The School of Salerno

Ah, nothing is too late,
Till the tired heart shall cease to palpitate.
Cato learned Greek at eighty; Sophocles
Wrote his grand Oedipus, and Simonides

Bore off the prize of verse from his compeers,
When each had numbered more than fourscore years.

Morituri Salutamus (1875)
Stanza 22

Turn, turn, my wheel! 'Tis nature's plan
The child should grow into the man.

Keramos (1878)

The holiest of all holidays are those
Kept by ourselves in silence and apart;
The secret anniversaries of the heart.

Holidays

There was a little girl
Who had a little curl
Right in the middle of her forehead;
And when she was good
She was very, very good,
But when she was bad she was horrid.

There Was a Little Girl

JOHN GREENLEAF WHITTIER
(1807-1892)

The Present, the Present is all thou hast
For thy sure possessing;
Like the patriarch's angel hold it fast
Till it gives its blessing

My Soul and I, Stanza 34

Art's perfect forms no moral need,
And Beauty is its own excuse;
But for the dull and flowerless weed
Some healing virtue still must plead.

Songs of Labor (1850)
Dedication, Stanza 5

From those great eyes
The soul has fled:
When faith is lost, when honor dies,
The man is dead!

Ichabod (1850), Stanza 8

For of all sad words of tongue or pen,
The saddest are these: "It might have been."

Maud Muller (1856) Stanza 53

Others shall sing the song,
Others shall right the wrong,—
Finish what I begin,
And all I fail of win.

My Triumph, Stanza 10

SAMUEL FRANCIS SMITH
(1808-1895)

My country, 'tis of thee,
Sweet land of liberty,
Of thee I sing:
Land where my fathers died.
Land of the pilgrims' pride,
From every mountain-side
Let freedom ring.

America (1831)

Our fathers' God, to thee,
Author of liberty,
To thee I sing;
Long may our land be bright
With freedom's holy light;
Protect us by thy might,
Great God, our King!

America

CHARLES ROBERT DARWIN
(1809-1882)

I have called this principle, by which each slight variation, if useful, is preserved, by the term Natural Selection.

The Origin of Species (1859)
Chap. 3

The expression often used by Mr. Herbert Spencer, of the Survival of the Fittest, is more accurate, and is sometimes equally convenient.

The Origin of Species (1859)
Chap. 3

The Simiadae then branched off into two great stems, the New World and Old World monkeys; and from the latter at a remote period, Man, the wonder and the glory of the universe, proceeded.

The Descent of Man. Chap. 6

I love fools' experiments. I am always making them.

Remark cited in Life of Darwin

EDWARD FITZGERALD
(1809-1883)

Awake! for Morning in the Bowl of Night
Has flung the Stone that puts the Stars to flight:
And Lo! the Hunter of the East has caught
The Sultan's Turret in a Noose of Light.

The Rubaiyat of Omar Khayyam
Stanza I, First Edition

Come, fill the Cup, and in the fire of Spring
Your Winter-garment of Repentance fling:
The Bird of Time has but a little way
To flutter—and the Bird is on the Wing.

The Rubaiyat of Omar Khayyam
Stanza 7

The Leaves of Life keep falling one by one.

The Rubaiyat of Omar Khayyam
Stanza 8

There was the Door to which I found no Key;
There was the Veil through which I might not see.
Some little talk awhile of Me and Thee
There was—and then no more of Thee and Me.

The Rubaiyat of Omar Khayyam
Stanza 32

The Moving Finger writes; and, having writ,
Moves on: nor all your Piety nor Wit

Shall lure it back to cancel half a Line,
Nor all your Tears wash out a Word of it.
The Rubaiyat of Omar Khayyam
Stanza 71

The King in a carriage may ride,
And the Beggar may crawl at his side;
But in the general race,
They are traveling all the same pace.

Chronomoros

OLIVER WENDELL HOLMES
(1809-1894)

Ay, tear her tattered ensign down!
Long has it waved on high,
And many an eye has danced to see
That banner in the sky.
Old Ironsides (1830) Stanza I

WILLIAM EWART GLADSTONE
(1809-1898)

National injustice is the surest road to national downfall.
Speech, Plumstead (1878)
All the world over, I will back the masses against the classes.
Speech, Liverpool (June 28, 1886)
Selfishness is the greatest curse of the human race.
Speech, Hawarden (May 28, 1890)

One sad, ungathered rose
On my ancestral tree.

My Aunt. Stanza 6

The lusty days of long ago,
When you were Bill and I was Joe.

Bill and Joe. Stanza I

Where the snow-flakes fall thickest there's nothing can freeze!
The Boys. Stanza 2

One flag, one land, one heart, one hand,
One Nation, evermore.

Voyage of the Good Ship Union.
Stanza 12

Put not your trust in money, but put your money in trust.

The Autocrat of the Breakfast-Table. I

The axis of the earth sticks out visibly through the centre of each and every town or city.

The Autocrat of the Breakfast-Table. VI

Have you heard of the wonderful one-hoss shay,
That was built in such a logical way
It ran a hundred years to a day?

The Deacon's Masterpiece (1858)
Stanza I

To be seventy years young is sometimes far more cheerful and hopeful than to be forty years old.

On the Seventieth Birthday of
Julia Ward Howe (May 27, 1889)

ABRAHAM LINCOLN
(1809-1865)

If destruction be our lot we must ourselves be its author and finisher. As a nation of freemen we must live through all time, or die by suicide.

Address, Young Men's Lyceum,
Springfield, Illinois
(January 27, 1838)

There is no grievance that is a fit object of redress by mob law.

Address, Young Men's Lyceum,
Springfield, Illinois
(January 27, 1838)

I am not a Know-Nothing; that is certain. How could I be? How can any one who abhors the oppression of Negroes be in favor of degrading classes of white people? Our progress in degeneracy appears to me to be pretty rapid. As a nation we began by declaring that "all men are created equal." We now practically read it "all men are created equal, except Negroes."

When the Know-Nothings get control, it will read "all men are created equal, except Negroes and foreigners, and Catholics." When it comes to this, I shall prefer emigrating to some country where they make no pretense of loving liberty—to Russia, for instance, where despotism can be taken pure, and without the base alloy of hypocrisy.

Letter to Joshua F. Speed
(August 24, 1855)

"A house divided against itself cannot stand." I believe this government cannot endure permanently half slave and half free. I do not expect the Union to be dissolved—I do not expect the house to fall—but I do expect it will cease to be divided. It will become all one thing, or all the other. Either the opponents of slavery will arrest the further spread of it, and place it where the public mind shall rest in the belief that it is in the course of ultimate extinction; or its advocates will push it forward till it shall become alike lawful in all the States, old as well as new, North as well as South.

Speech, Republican State
Convention, Springfield, Illinois
(June 16, 1858)

As I would not be a *slave*, so I would not be a *master*. This expresses my idea of democracy. Whatever differs from this, to the extent of the difference, is no democracy.

Fragment (August 1, 1858?) in
Roy P. Basler: The Collected
Works of Abraham Lincoln
(1952. Vol. II, Page 532)

This is a world of compensation; and he who would be no slave must consent to have no slave. Those who deny freedom to others deserve it not for themselves, and, under a just God, cannot long retain it.

Letter to H.L. Pierce and
Others (April 6, 1859)

Let us have faith that right makes might, and in that faith let us to the end dare to do our duty as we understand it.

Address, Cooper Union, New York
(February 27, 1860)

Fourscore and seven years ago our fathers brought forth on this continent a new nation, conceived in liberty, and dedicated to the proposition that all men are created equal.

Now we are engaged in a great civil war, testing whether that nation, or any nation so conceived and so dedicated, can long endure. We are met on a great battlefield of that war. We have come to dedicate a portion of that field as a final resting-place for those who here gave their lives that that nation might live. It is altogether fitting and proper that we should do this.

But, in a larger sense, we cannot dedicate—we cannot consecrate—we cannot hallow—this ground. The brave men, living and dead, who struggled here, have consecrated it far above our poor power to add or detract. The world will little note nor long remember what we say here, but it can never forget what they did here. It is for us, the living, rather to be dedicated here to the unfinished work which they who fought here have thus far so nobly advanced. It is rather for us to be here dedicated to the great task remaining before us—that from these honored dead we take increased devotion to that cause for which they gave the last full measure of devotion; that we here highly resolve that these dead shall not have died in vain; that this nation, under God, shall have a new birth of freedom; and that government of the people, by the people, for the people shall not perish from the earth.

Address of Gettysburg
(November 19, 1863)

Truth is generally the best vindication against slander.

Letter to Secretary Stanton,
refusing to dismiss Postmaster-
General Montgomery Blair
(July 18, 1864)

With malice toward none; with charity for all; with firmness in the right, as God gives us to see the right, let us strive on to finish the work we are in; to bind up the nation's wounds; to care for him who shall have borne the battle, and for his widow, and his orphan—to do all which may achieve and cherish a just and lasting peace among ourselves, and with all nations.

Second Inaugural Address
(March 4, 1865)

If you call a tail a leg, how many legs has a dog? Five? No, calling a tail a leg doesn't *make* it a leg.

Traditionally attributed to Lincoln

RICHARD MONCKTON MILNES (BARON HOUGHTON) (1809-1885)

The beating of my own heart
Was all the sound I heard.

The Brookside, Stanza 1

A fair little girl sat under a tree,
Sewing as long as her eyes could see;
Then smoothed her work, and folded it right,
And said, "Dear work, good-night, good-night."

Good-Night and Good-Morning.
Stanza 1

EDGAR ALLAN POE (1809-1849)

All that we see or seem
Is but a dream within a dream.

A Dream Within a Dream (1827)

There are chords in the hearts of the most reckless which can not be touched without emotion. Even with the utterly lost, to whom life and death are equally jests, there are matters of which no jest can be made.

The Masque of the Red Death (1842)

While the angels, all pallid and wan,
Uprising, unveiling, affirm
That the play is the tragedy, "Man,"
And its hero, the Conqueror Worm.

The Conqueror Worm. Stanza 5

Once upon a midnight dreary, while I pondered,
weak and weary,

Over many a quaint and curious volume of forgotten
lore—
While I nodded, nearly napping, suddenly there came
a tapping,
As of some one gently rapping, rapping at my chamber
door.

The Raven (1845) Stanza 1

Ah, distinctly I remember it was in the bleak December;
And each separate dying ember wrought its ghost upon
the floor.
Eagerly I wished the morrow;—vainly I had sought to
borrow
From my books surcease of sorrow—
sorrow for the lost Lenore—
For the rare and radiant maiden whom
the angels name Lenore—
Nameless *here* for evermore.

The Raven, Stanza 2

"Ghastly grim and ancient Raven wandering from the
Nightly shore—
Tell me what thy lordly name is on the Night's Plutonian
shore!"
Quoth the Raven, "Nevermore."

The Raven, Stanza 8

And the Raven, never flitting, still is sitting, still is
sitting, *still* is sitting
On the pallid bust of Pallas just above my chamber door;
And his eyes have all the seeming of a demon's that is
dreaming,
And the lamp-light o'er him streaming throws his shadow
on the floor;
And my soul from out that shadow that lies floating on
the floor;
And my soul from out that shadow that lies floating on the floor
Shall be lifted—nevermore!

The Raven, Stanza 18

And the fever called "living"
Is conquered at last.

For Annie (1849)

She was a child and *I* was a child,
In this kingdom by the sea,
But we loved with a love that was more than love—
I and my Annabel Lee—
With a love that the winged seraphs of Heaven
Coveted her and me.

Annabel Lee (1849) Stanza 1

And neither the angels in Heaven above
Nor the demons down under the sea,
Can ever dissever my soul from the soul
Of the beautiful Annabel Lee.

Annabel Lee (1849) Stanza 5

ALFRED, LORD TENNYSON
(1809-1892)

Dowered with the hate of hate, the scorn of scorn,
The love of love.

The Poet (1830) Stanza 1

A still small voice spake unto me,
"Thou art so full of misery,
Were it not better not to be?"

The Two Voices (1833) Stanza 1

No life that breathes with human breath
Has ever truly longed for death.

The Two Voices (1833) Stanza 132

Self-reverence, self-knowledge, self-control,
These three alone lead life to sovereign power.

Oenone (1833) Line 142

A simple maiden in her flower
Is worth a hundred coats-of-arms.

Lady Clara Vere de Vere (1833)
Stanza 2

If time be heavy on your hands,
Are there no beggars at your gate,

Nor any poor about your lands?
Oh! teach the orphan-boy to read,
Or teach the orphan-girl to sew.

Lady Clara Vere de Vere, Stanza 9

There is sweet music here that softer falls
Than petals from blown roses on the grass.

The Lotos-Eaters (1833) Choric
Song, Stanza 1

The old order changeth, yielding place to new;
And God fulfills himself in many ways,
Lest one good custom should corrupt the world.

Morte d'Arthur (1842) Line 408

Ah! when shall all men's good
Be each man's rule, and universal peace
Lie like a shaft of light across the land?

The Golden Year (1842) Line 47

My strength is as the strength of ten,
Because my heart is pure.

Sir Galahad (1842) Stanza 1

Sweet and low, sweet and low,
Wind of the western sea,
Low, low, breathe and blow,
Wind of the western sea!
Over the rolling waters go,
Come from the dying moon, and blow,
Blow him again to me;
While my little one, while my pretty
one, sleeps.

The Princess, Part III, Song

Man is the hunter; woman is his game.

The Princess, Part V, Line 147

Man for the field and woman for the hearth:
Man for the sword and for the needle she:
Man with the head and woman with the heart:
Man to command and woman to obey;
All else confusion.

The Princess, Part V, Line 427

And Thought leapt out to wed with Thought
Ere Thought could wed itself with Speech.

In Memoriam, Part XXIII, Stanza 4

'Tis better to have loved and lost
Than never to have loved at all.

In Memoriam. Part XXIII, Stanza 4

But what am I?
An infant crying in the night:
An infant crying for the light:
And with no language but a cry.

In Memoriam. Part LIV, Stanza 5

God's finger touch'd him, and he slept.

In Memoriam. Part LXXXV, Stanza 5

There lives more faith in honest doubt,
Believe me, than in half the creeds.

In Memoriam. Part XCVI, Stanza 3

He seems so near, and yet so far.

In Memoriam. Part XCVII, Stanza 6

Ring out, wild bells, to the wild sky!

In Memoriam. Part CVI, Stanza 1

Ring out the old, ring in the new,
Ring, happy bells, across the snow!

In Memoriam. Part CVI, Stanza 2

Half a league, half a league,
Half a league onward,
All in the valley of death
Rode the six hundred.

The Charge of the Light Brigade
(1854) Stanza 1

Some one had blundered:
Theirs not to make reply,
Theirs not to reason why,
Theirs but to do and die.

The Charge of the Light Brigade
(1854) Stanza 2

Cannon to right of them,
Cannon to left of them,

Cannon in front of them
Volley'd and thunder'd . . . .
Into the jaws of death,
Into the mouth of hell
Rode the six hundred.

The Charge of the Light Brigade
(1854) Stanza 3

She is coming, my own, my sweet,
Were it ever so airy a tread,
My heart would hear her and beat,
Were it earth in an earthy bed;
My dust would hear her and beat,
Had I lain for a century dead;
Would start and tremble under her feet,
And blossom in purple and red.

Maud, Part I, XXII, Stanza 11

For man is man and master of his fate.

Idylls of the King. The Marriage
of Geraint, Line 355

That a lie which is half a truth is ever
the blackest of lies,
That a lie which is all a lie may be met
and fought with outright,
But a lie which is part a truth is a
harder matter to fight.

The Grandmother (1864) Stanza 8

Flower in the crannied wall,
I pluck you out of the crannies,
I hold you here, root and all, in my hand,
Little flower—but *if* I could understand
What you are, root and all, and all in all,
I should know what God and man is.

Flower in the Crannied Wall (1869)

SAMUEL DODGE
(Circa 1868)

You may go through this world, but 'twill be very slow

If you listen to all that is said as you go;
You'll be worried and fretted and kept in a stew,
For meddlesome tongues must have something to do,
For people will talk, you know.

People Will Talk, Stanza 1

PHINEAS TAYLOR BARNUM
(1810-1891)

There's a sucker born every minute.

Attributed

WILLIAM HENRY CHANNING
(1810-1884)

To live content with small means; to seek elegance rather than
luxury, and refinement rather than fashion; to be worthy, not
respectable, and wealthy, not rich; to study hard, think quietly,
talk gently, act frankly; to listen to stars and birds, to babes and
sages, with open heart; to bear all cheerfully, do all bravely,
await occasions, hurry never. In a word, to let the spiritual un-
bidden and unconscious, grow up through the common. This is
to be my symphony.

My Symphony

DANIEL CLEMENT COLESWORTHY
(1810-1893)

A little word in kindness spoken,
A motion or a tear,
Has often healed the heart that's broken,
And made a friend sincere.

A Little Word. Stanza 1

Then deem it not an idle thing
A pleasant word to speak;
The face you wear—the thoughts you bring—
The heart may heal or break.

A Little Word. Stanza 3

JAMES SLOANE GIBBONS
(1810-1892)

We are coming, Father Abraham, three
hundred thousand more,
From Mississippi's winding stream and
from New England's shore;
We leave our ploughs and workshops,
our wives and children dear,
With hearts too full for utterance, with
but a silent tear.

Three Hundred Thousand More,
Stanza 1

WILLIAM MILLER
(1810-1872)

Wee Willie Winkie rins through the toun,
Upstairs and dounstairs, in his nichtgoun,
Tirlin' at the window, cryin' at the lock,
"Are the weans in their bed? for it's nou ten o'clock."

Willie Winkie

THEODORE PARKER
(1810-1860)

Truth never yet fell dead in the streets; it has such
affinity with the soul of man, the seed however broadcast
will catch somewhere and produce its hundredfold.

A Discourse of Matters Pertaining
to Religion (1842)

Truth stood on one side and Ease on the other; it has often
been so.

A Discourse of Matters
Pertaining to Religion (1842)

Man never falls so low that he can see nothing higher than
himself.

Essay, A Lesson for the Day

All men desire to be immortal.

> *A Sermon on the Immortal Life*
> *(September 20, 1846)*

HORACE GREELEY
(1811-1872)

A widow of doubtful age will marry almost any sort of a white man.

> *Letter to Dr. Rufus Wilmot*
> *Griswold*

If, on a full and final review, my life and practice shall be found unworthy of my principles, let due infamy be heaped on my memory; but let none be thereby led to distrust the principles to which I proved recreant, nor yet the ability of some to adorn them by a suitable life and conversation. To unerring time be all this committed.

> *Statement (1846) quoted in*
> *James Parton: Life of Horace*
> *Greeley (1855)*

The best business you can go into you will find on your father's farm or in his workshop. If you have no family or friends to aid you, and no prospect opened to you there, turn your face to the great West, and there build up a home and fortune.

> *To Aspiring Young Men. Page 414*

The illusion that times that were are better than those that are, has probably pervaded all ages.

> *The American Conflict (1864-1866)*

FRANCES SARGENT OSGOOD
(1811-1850)

Work—for some good, be it ever so slowly;
Cherish some flower, be it ever so lowly;
Labor!—all labor is noble and holy!
Let thy great deeds be thy prayer to thy God!

> *Laborare est Orare. Stanza 6*

WENDELL PHILLIPS
(1811-1884)

Revolutions are not made; they come. A revolution is as natural a growth as an oak. It comes out of the past. Its foundations are laid far back.

Speech (January 28, 1852)

The best use of laws is to teach men to trample bad laws under their feet.

Speech (April 12, 1852)

What the Puritans gave the world was not thought, but action.

Speech (December 21, 1855)

One on God's side is a majority.

Speech (November 1, 1859)

Every man meets his Waterloo at last.

Speech (November 1, 1859)

Some doubt the courage of the Negro. Go to Haiti and stand on those fifty thousand graves of the best soldiers France ever had, and ask them what they think of the Negro's sword.

Address on Toussaint L'Ouverture
(1861)

Aristocracy is always cruel.

Address on Toussaint L'Ouverture
(1861)

HARRIET BEECHER STOWE
(1811-1896)

I 'spect I growed. Don't think nobody never made me.

Uncle Tom's Cabin (1852) Chap. 20

I's wicked—I is. I's mighty wicked, anyhow. I can't help it.

Uncle Tom's Cabin (1852) Chap. 20

It lies around us like a cloud,
A world we do not see;
Yet the sweet closing of an eye
May bring us there to be.

The Other World (1867) Stanza 1

WILLIAM MAKEPEACE THACKERAY
(1811-1863)

The play is done; the curtain drops,
Slow falling to the prompter's bell:
A moment yet the actor stops,
And looks around, to say farewell.
It is an irksome word and task;
And when he's laughed and said his say,
He shows, as he removes the mask,
A face that's anything but gay.

> *Doctor Birch and His Young Friends.*
> *Epilogue, The End of the Play*
> *Stanza 1*

Though more than half the world was his,
He died without a rood his own;
And borrow'd from his enemies
Six foot of ground to lie upon.

> *The Chronicle of the Drum. Part II*

Away from the world and its toils and its cares,
I've a snug little kingdom up four pairs of stairs.

> *The Cane-Bottom'd Chair. Stanza 1*

The rose upon my balcony the morning air
perfuming,
Was leafless all the winter time and pining
for the spring.

> *The Rose Upon My Balcony. Stanza 1*

In the brave days when I was twenty-one.

> *The Garret, Refrain*

Them's my sentiments.

> *Vanity Fair (1847-1849)*
> *Vol. 1, Chap. 21*

When we say of a gentleman that he lives elegantly on nothing
a year, we use the word "nothing" to signify something unknown; meaning, simply, that we don't know how the
gentleman in question defrays the expenses of his establish-
ment.

> *Vanity Fair. Vol. I, Chap. 35*

Ah! *Vanitas Vanitatum!* Which of us is happy in this world?
Which of us has his desire? or, having it, is satisfied?
—Come, children, let us shut up the box and the puppets,
for our play is played out.

Vanity Fair. Vol. II, Chap. 27

Remember, it's as easy to marry a rich woman as a poor woman.

Pendennis. Chap. 28

"Tis not the dying for a faith that's so hard, Master Harry—every
man of every nation has done that—'tis the living up to it that's
difficult."

Henry Esmond (1852) Book I, Chap. 6

'Tis strange what a man may do, and a woman yet think him an
angel.

Henry Esmond (1852) Book I, Chap. 7

A pedigree reaching as far back as the Deluge.

The Rose and the Ring (1855) Chap. 2

Heaven does not choose its elect from among the great and
wealthy.

The Virginians (1857-1859) Chap. 5

Bravery never goes out of fashion.

The Four Georges (1860) George II

ROBERT BROWNING
(1812-1889)

Any nose
May ravage with impunity a rose.

Sordello (1840) VI

Day!
Faster and more fast,
O'er night's brim, day boils at last.

Pippa Passes (1841) Introduction

The year's at the spring
And day's at the morn;
Morning's at seven;
The hillside's dew-pearled;
The lark's on the wing;

The snail's on the thorn:
God's in his heaven—
All's right with the world.

Pippa Passes (1841) Part I

Marching along, fifty-score strong,
Great hearted gentlemen, singing this song.

Bells and Pomegranates (1841-1846)
Cavalier Tunes, I, Marching Along

Boot, saddle, to horse, and away!

Bells and Pomegranates (1841-1846)
Cavalier Tunes, III, Boot and Saddle

Where the apple reddens
Never pry—
Lest we lose our Edens,
Eve and I.

Bells and Pomegranates.
A Woman's Last Word, Stanza 5

That shall be tomorrow
Not tonight:
I must bury sorrow
Out of sight.

Bells and Pomegranates.
A Woman's Last Word, Stanza 9

That's the wise thrush; he sings each song twice over,
Lest you should think he never could recapture
The first fine careless rapture!

Bells and Pomegranates. Home-
Thoughts, from Abroad, Stanza 2

Escape me?
Never—
Beloved!
While I am I, and you are you.

Belles and Pomegranates. Life in
a Love, Stanza I

The lie was dead,
And damned, and truth stood up instead.

Bells and Pomegranates.
Count Gismond, Stanza 13

Rats!
They fought the dogs and killed the cats,
And bit the babies in the cradles,
And ate the cheeses out of the vats,
And licked the soup from the cooks' own ladles.

Bells and Pomegranates.
The Pied Piper of Hamelin, Stanza 2

Ah, but a man's reach should exceed his grasp,
Or what's a heaven for.

Men and Women (1855), Andrea del Sarto

You call for faith:
I show you doubt, to prove that faith exists.
The more of doubt, the stronger faith, I say,
If faith o'ercomes doubt.

Men and Women. Bishop Blougram's
Apology

When the fight begins within himself,
A man's worth something.

Men and Women. Bishop Blougram's
Apology

Grow old along with me!
The best is yet to be,
The last of life, for which the first was made.
Our times are in his hand.

Dramatis Personae. Rabbi Ben Ezra
Stanza I

How sad and bad and mad it was—
But then, how it was sweet!

Dramatis Personae. Confessions
Stanza 9

It's wiser being good than bad;
It's safer being meek than fierce;
It's fitter being sane than mad.
My own hope is, a sun will pierce
The thickest cloud earth ever stretched;
That, after Last, returns the First,
Though a wide compass round be fetched;

That what began best can't end worst,
Nor what God blessed once, prove accurst.

> *Dramatis Personae. Apparent*
> *Failure, Stanza 7*

You never know what life means till you die:
Even throughout life, 'tis death that makes life live,
Gives it whatever the significance.

> *The Ring and the Book, XI, Guido*

CHARLES DICKENS
(1812-1870)

There are books of which the backs and covers are by far the best parts.

> *Oliver Twist (1837-1838) Chap. 2*

"If the law supposes that," said Mr. Bumble, ". . . the law is a ass, a idiot."

> *Oliver Twist (1837-1838) Chap. 51*

He had but one eye, and the popular prejudice runs in favour of two.

> *Nicholas Nickleby (1838-1839)*
> *Chap. 4*

Subdue your appetites, my dears, and you've conquered human natur.

> *Nicholas Nickleby (1838-1839)*
> *Chap. 5*

There are only two styles of portrait painting, the serious and the smirk.

> *Nicholas Nickleby (1838-1839)*
> *Chap. 10*

Oh! they're too beautiful to live, much too beautiful!

> *Nicholas Nickleby (1838-1839)*
> *Chap. 14*

Bring in the bottled lightning, a clean tumbler, and a cork-screw.

> *Nicholas Nickleby. Chap. 49*

The memory of those who lie below passes away so soon. At first they tend them, morning, noon, and night; they soon begin to come less frequently; from once a day, to once a week; from once a week to once a month; then at long and uncertain intervals, then, not at all.

The Old Curiosity Shop (1841)
Chap. 54

It was a maxim with Foxey—our revered father, gentlemen—"Always suspect everybody."

The Old Curiosity Shop (1841)
Chap. 66

Oh gracious, why wasn't I born old and ugly?

Barnaby Rudge (1841) Chap. 70

Regrets are the natural property of gray hairs.

Martin Chuzzlewit (1843-1844)
Chap. 10

Keep up appearances whatever you do.

Martin Chuzzlewit (1843-1844)
Chap. 11

"Do other men for they would do you." That's the true business precept.

Martin Chuzzlewit (1843-1844)
Chap. 11

Let's have the shutters up . . . before a man can say Jack Robinson.

A Christmas Carol (1843) Stave Two

It's a mad world. Mad as Bedlam.

David Copperfield, Chap. 14

I'm a very umble person.

David Copperfield, Chap. 16

There wasn't room to swing a cat there.

David Copperfield, Chap. 35

I ate umble pie with an appetite.

David Copperfield, Chap. 39

A man must take the fat with the lean.

David Copperfield, Chap. 51

Trifles make the sum of life.

David Copperfield, Chap. 53

It was the best of times, it was the worst of times, it was the age of wisdom, it was the age of foolishness, it was the epoch of belief, it was the epoch of incredulity, it was the season of Light, it was the season of Darkness, it was the spring of hope, it was the winter of despair.

A Tale of Two Cities (1859)
Book I, Chap. 6

EDWARD LEAR
(1812-1888)

There was an Old Man with a beard,
Who said: "It is just as I feared!
Two Owls and a Hen,
Four Larks and a Wren
Have all built their nests in my beard."

Book of Nonsense (1846). Limerick

How pleasant to know Mr. Lear!
Who has written such volumes of stuff!
Some think him ill-tempered and queer,
But a few think him pleasant enough.

Nonsense Songs (1871)
Preface, Stanza 1

The Owl and the Pussy-cat went to sea
In a beautiful pea-green boat,
They took some honey, and plenty of money,
Wrapped up in a five-pound note.
The Owl looked up to the stars above,
And sang to a small guitar,
"O lovely Pussy! O Pussy, my love,
What a beautiful Pussy you are,
You are,
You are!
What a beautiful Pussy you are!"

Nonsense Songs. The Owl and the
Pussy-cat, Stanza 1

NORMAN MACLEOD
(1812-1872)

Courage, brother! do not stumble,
Though thy   path be dark as night;
There's a star to guide the humble,
Trust in God and do the Right.

Trust in God (1857) Stanza 1

HENRY WARD BEECHER
(1813-1887)

A thoughtful mind, when it sees a Nation's flag, sees not the
flag only, but the Nation itself; and whatever may be its sym-
bols, its insignia, he reads chiefly in the flag the Government,
the principles, the truths, the history which belongs to the Nation that sets it forth.

The American Flag

JOHN SULLIVAN DWIGHT
(1813-1893)

Is not true leisure
One with true toil?

Rest. Stanza 1

Rest is not quitting
The busy career,
Rest is the fitting
Of self to its sphere.

Rest. Stanza 4

FREDERICK WILLIAM FABER
(1814-1863)

The sea, unmated creature, tired and lone,
Makes on its desolate sands eternal moan.•

The Sorrowful World

O Paradise! O Paradise!
Who doth not crave for rest?

Who would not seek the happy land
Where they that love are blest?

Paradise

CHARLES MACKAY
(1814-1889)

Cannon-balls may aid the truth,
But thought's a weapon stronger;
We'll win our battles by its aid;—
Wait a little longer.

The Good Time Coming. Stanza I

The smallest effort is not lost,
Each wavelet on the ocean tost
Aids in the ebb-tide or the flow;
Each rain-drop makes some floweret blow;
Each struggle lessens human woe.

The Old and the New

There is no such thing as death.
In Nature nothing dies.
From each sad remnant of decay
Some forms of life arise.

There Is No Such Thing as Death

MICHAEL WENTWORTH BECK
(1815-1843)

This world is not so bad a world
As some would like to make it;
Though whether good, or whether bad,
Depends on how we take it.

The World As It Is. Stanza 1

DANIEL DECATUR EMMETT
(1815-1904)

I wish I was in de land ob cotton,
Old times dar am not forgotten.

Look away, look away,
Look away, Dixie Land.

Dixie (1859)

In Dixie's land, we'll took our stand,
To lib an' die in Dixie!
Away, away,
Away down South in Dixie.

Dixie (1859)

PHILIP JAMES BAILEY
(1816-1902)

Let each man think himself an act of God,
His mind a thought, his life a breath of God;
And let each try, by great thoughts and good deeds,
To show the most of Heaven he hath in him.

Festus (1839). Proem

CHARLOTTE BRONTE
(1816-1855)

The human heart has hidden treasures,
In secret kept, in silence sealed;—
The thoughts, the hopes, the dreams, the pleasures,
Whose charms were broken if revealed.

Evening Solace (1845) Stanza I

JOHN GODFREY SAXE
(1816-1887)

I'm growing fonder of my staff;
I'm growing dimmer in the eyes;
I'm growing fainter in my laugh;
I'm growing deeper in my sighs;
I'm growing careless of my dress;
I'm growing frugal of my gold;
I'm growing wise; I'm growing—yes,—
I'm growing old!

I'm Growing Old. Stanza 3

HENRY DAVID THOREAU
(1817-1862)

Any man more right than his neighbors constitutes a majority of one.

Civil Disobedience (1849)

It takes two to speak the truth,—one to speak, and another to hear.

*A Week on the Concord and
Merrimack Rivers (1849) Wednesday*

Nothing is so much to be feared as fear.

Journal. September, 1850

When the playful breeze drops in the pool, it springs to right and left, quick as a kitten playing with dead leaves.

Journal. April 9, 1859

The savage in man is never quite eradicated.

Journal. September 26, 1859

Public opinion is a weak tyrant compared with our own private opinion. What a man thinks of himself, that it is which determines, or rather indicates, his fate.

Walden. I, Economy

The mass of men   lead lives of quiet desperation.

Walden. I, Economy

There is no odor so bad as that which arises from goodness tainted.

Walden. I, Economy

How many a man has dated a new era in his life from the reading of a book.

Walden. III, Reading

I love a broad margin to my life.

Walden. IV, Sounds

Our horizon is never quite at our elbows.

Walden. V, Solitude

EMILY BRONTE
(1818-1848)

Sleep not, dream not; this bright day

Will not, cannot last for aye;
Bliss like thine is bought by years
Dark with torment and with tears.

Sleep Not (1846) Stanza 1

I lingered round them, under that benign sky: watched the
moths fluttering among the heath and hare-bells; listened to
the soft wind breathing through the grass; and wondered how
any one could ever imagine unquiet slumbers for the sleepers
in that quiet earth.

Wuthering Heights (1846) Last Words

KARL MARX
(1818-1883)

Religion . . . is the opium of the people.

*Critique of the Hegelian Philosophy
of Right (1844) Introduction*

The history of all hitherto existing society is the history of class
struggles.

*Manifesto of the Communist Party
(1848) I*

The proletarians have nothing to lose but their chains. They
have a world to win. Workers of the world, unite!

*Manifesto of the Communist Party
(1848) IV*

From each according to his abilities, to each according to his
needs.

Critique of the Gotha Program (1875)

IVAN SERGEYEVICH TURGENIEV
(1818-1883)

That air of superiority to the rest of the world which usually dis-
appears when once the twenties have been passed.

Fathers and Sons (1862), Chap. 4

A picture may instantly present what a book could set forth
only in a hundred pages.

Fathers and Sons, Chap. 16

GEORGE ELIOT
(MARIAN EVANS CROSS)
(1819-1880)

'Tis God gives skill,
But not without men's hands: He could not make
Antonio Stradivari's violins
Without Antonio.

Stradivarius

He was like a cock who thought the sun had risen to hear him
crow.

Adam Bede (1859) Chap. 33

Blessed is the man who, having nothing to say, abstains from
giving in words evidence of the fact.

Impressions of Theophrastus
Such (1879)

JOSIAH GILBERT HOLLAND
(1819-1881)

Heaven is not reached at a single bound;
But we build the ladder by which we rise
From the lowly earth to the vaulted skies,
And we mount to its summit round by round.

Gradatim. Stanza I

God give us men! A time like this demands
Strong minds, great hearts, true faith, and ready hands;
Men whom the lust of office does not kill;
Men whom the spoils of office cannot buy;
Men who possess opinions and a will;
Men who have honor; men who will not lie.

The Day's Demand

JULIA WARD HOWE
(1819-1910)

Mine eyes have seen the glory of the coming of the Lord;
He is trampling out the vintage where the grapes of
wrath are stored;

He hath loosed the fateful lightning of His terrible,
swift sword;
His truth is marching on.

Battle Hymn of the Republic
(1862) Stanza I

CHARLES KINGSLEY
(1819-1875)

Thank God every morning when you get up that you have
something to do that day which must be done, whether you
like it or not. Being forced to work and forced to do your best,
will breed in you temperance and self-control, diligence and
strength of will, cheerfulness and content, and a hundred virtues which the idle never know.

Town and Country Sermons (1861)

Some say that the age of chivalry is past, that the spirit of
romance is dead. The age of chivalry is never past, so long as
there is a wrong left unredressed on earth.

Life (1879) Vol. II, Chap. 28

JAMES RUSSELL LOWELL
(1819-1891)

Great Truths are portions of the soul of man;
Great souls are portions of Eternity.

Sonnet VI (1841)

His words were simple words enough,
And yet he used them so,
That what in other mouths was rough
In his seemed musical and low.

The Shepherd of King Admetus
(1842) Stanza 5

No man is born into the world whose work
Is not born with him; there is always work,
And tools to work withal, for those who will;
And blessed are the horny hands of toil.

A Glance Behind the Curtain (1843)

Once to every man and nation comes the
moment to decide,
In the strife of Truth with Falsehood,
for the good or evil side.

The Present Crisis (1844)
Stanza 5

The birch, most shy and ladylike of trees.

An Indian-Summer Reverie (1846)
Stanza 8

And what is so rare as a day in June?
Then, if ever, come perfect days;
Then Heaven tries the earth if it be in tune,
And over it softly her warm ear lays.

The Vision of Sir Launfal (1848)
Part I, Prelude, Stanza 5

Slowly the Bible of the race is writ,
And not on paper leaves nor leaves of stone;
Each age, each kindred, adds a verse to it,
Texts of despair or hope, of joy or moan.

Bibliolatres (1849) Stanza 6

Talent is that which is in a man's power; genius is that in whose
power a man is.

Rousseau and the Sentimentalists

Every man feels instinctively that all the beautiful sentiments in
the world weigh less than a single lovely action.

Rousseau and the Sentimentalists

There is no good in arguing with the inevitable. The only argument available with an east wind is to put on your overcoat.

Democracy and Addresses

HERMAN MELVILLE
(1819-1891)

Sailor or landsman, there is some sort of Cape Horn for all.
Boys! beware of it; prepare for it in time. Greybeards! thank
God it is passed.

White-Jacket (1850) Chap. 26

A whale ship was my Yale College and my Harvard
Moby Dick. Chap. 24

All dies! and not alone
The aspiring trees and men and grass;
The poets' forms of beauty pass,
And noblest deeds they are undone,
Even truth itself decays, and lo,
From truth's sad ashes pain and falsehood grow.
The Lake

JOHN RUSKIN
(1819-1900)

He is the greatest artist who has embodied, in the sum of his works, the greatest number of the greatest ideas.
Modern Painters. Vol. I (1843)
Part I, Chap. 2, Sect. 9

The greatest thing a human soul ever does in this world is to *see* something, and tell what it *saw* in a plain way. Hundreds of people can talk for one who can think, but thousands can think for one who can see. To see clearly is poetry, prophecy, and religion, all in one.
Modern Painters. Vol. III (1856)
Part IV, Chap. 16, Sect. 28

Give a little love to a child, and you get a great deal back.
The Crown of Wild Olive (1866)
Work, Sect. 49

WILLIAM ROSS WALLACE
(1819-1881)

The hand that rocks the cradle is the hand
that rules the world.
The Hand That Rules the World
Stanza I

WALT WHITMAN
(1819-1892)

I believe a leaf of grass is no less than the journeywork of the stars.

Leaves of Grass. Song of Myself, 31

And the tree-toad is a chef-d'oeuvre
for the highest ....
And a mouse is miracle enough to stagger
sextillions of infidels.

Leaves of Grass. Song of Myself, 31

In the faces of men and women I see God.

Leaves of Grass. Song of Myself, 48

O Captain! my Captain! our fearful trip is done!
The ship has weather'd every rack
the prize we sought is won,
The port is near, the bells I hear, the
people all exulting.

Leaves of Grass. My Captain! I

To me every hour of the light and dark is a miracle,
Every cubic inch of space is a miracle.

Leaves of Grass. Miracles 2

There is no week nor day nor hour, when tyranny may not enter upon this country, if the people lose their roughness and spirit of defiance—Tyranny may always enter—there is no charm, no bar against it—the only bar against it is a large resolute breed of men.

Notes for Lecturers on
Democracy and "Adhesiveness."
C. J. Furness: Walt Whitman's
Workshop (1928)

GEORGE FREDERICK ROOT
(1820-1895)

Tramp! Tramp! Tramp! the boys are marching,
Cheer up, comrades, they will come,
And beneath the starry flag

We shall breathe the air again
Of the free land in our own beloved home.

Tramp! Tramp! Tramp! (1862)

JOHN TYNDALL
(1820-1893)

Life is a wave, which in no two consecutive moments of its existence is composed of the same particles.

Fragments of Science. Vol. II
Vitality

The brightest flashes in the world of thought are incomplete until they have been proved to have their counterparts in the world of fact.

Fragments of Science. Vol. II
Scientific Materialism

HERBERT SPENCER
(1820-1903)

Progress, therefore, is not an accident, but a necessity . . . .
It is a part of nature.

Social Statics (1851) Part I, Chap. 2

Morality knows nothing of geographical boundaries or distinction of race.

Social Statics. Part IV, Chap. 30

Music must take rank as the highest of the fine arts—as the one which, more than any other, ministers to human welfare.

Essays on Education (1861)
On the Origin and Function of
Music

Volumes might be written upon the impiety of the pious.

First Principles

This survival of the fittest.

Principles of Biology (1864-1869)
Part III, Chap. 12

The ultimate result of shielding men from the effects of folly is to fill the world with fools.

Essays (1891) Tamperings with
Money Banks

GEORGE JOHN WHYTE-MELVILLE
(1821-1878)

In the choice of a horse and a wife, a man must please himself, ignoring the opinion and advice of friends.

Riding Recollections (1878)

Education should be as gradual as the moonrise, perceptible not in progress but in result.

Riding Recollections (1878)

MARY BAKER EDDY
(1821-1910)

Divine Love always has met and always will meet every human need.

Science and Health with Key to
the Scriptures. Page 494

To live and let live, without clamor for distinction or recognition; to wait on divine Love; to write truth first on the tablet of one's own heart,—this is the sanity and perfection of living, and my human ideal.

Message to the Mother Church
for 1902. Page 2

FYODOR DOSTOYEVSKY
(1821-1881)

Man is a pliable animal, a being who gets accustomed to everything!

The House of the Dead (Prison
Life in Siberia, 1861-1862)
Part I, Chap. 2

Tyranny is a habit capable of being developed, and at last

becomes a disease . . . The man and the citizen disappear for ever in the tyrant.

The House of the Dead (Prison Life in Siberia). Part II, Chap. 3

Be not forgetful of prayer. Every time you pray, if your prayer is sincere, there will be new feeling and new meaning in it, which will give you fresh courage, and you will understand that prayer is an education.

The Brothers Karamazov (1880) Part II, Book VI, Chap. 3

Love all God's creation, the whole and every grain of sand in it. Love every leaf, every ray of God's light. Love the animals, love the plants, love everything. If you love everything, you will perceive the divine mystery in things. Once you perceive it, you will begin to comprehend it better every day. And you will come at last to love the whole world with an all-embracing love.

The Brothers Karamazov. Part II Book VI, Chap. 3

Men reject their prophets and slay them, but they love their martyrs and honour those whom they have slain.

The Brothers Karamazov. Part II Book VI, Chap. 3

CHARLES BAUDELAIRE
(1821-1867)

There are in every man, at every hour, two simultaneous postulations, one towards God, the other towards Satan.

Mon Coeur Mis a Nu (1887) XIX

There exist only three beings worthy of respect: the priest, the soldier, the poet. To know, to kill, to create.

Mon Coeur Mis a Nu (1887) XXII

To be a great man and a saint for oneself, that is the one important thing.

Mon Coeur Mis a Nu (1887) LII

ULYSSES S. GRANT
(1822-1885)

Leave the matter of religion to the family altar, the church, and the private school, supported entirely by private contributions. Keep the church and the State for ever separate.

Speech at Des Moines, Iowa (1875)

EDWARD EVERETT HALE
(1822-1909)

I am only one,
But still I am one.
I cannot do everything,
But still I can do something;
And because I cannot do everything
I will not refuse to do the something
that I can do.

For the Lend-a-Hand Society

To look up and not down,
To look forward and not back,
To look out and not in, and
To lend a hand.

Ten Times One Is Ten (1870)

BERNARD ELLIOTT BEE
(1823-1861)

See, there is Jackson, standing like a stone-wall.

*Of General T.J. Jackson, at the
Battle of Bull Run (July 21, 1861)*

WILLIAM BRIGHTY RANDS
("MATTHEW BROWNE")
(1823-1882)

Never do today what you can
Put off till tomorrow.

Lilliput Levee

FRANCIS PARKMAN
(1823-1893)

The French Revolution began at the top—in the world of fashion, birth, and intellect—and propagated itself downwards.

Montcalm and Wolfe (1884)
Introduction

EDWARD HAZEN PARKER
(1823-1896)

Life's race well run,
Life's work well done,
Life's victory won,
Now cometh rest.

Funeral Ode on James A. Garfield
Stanza I

EDWARD POLLOCK
(1823-1858)

There's something in the parting hour
Will chill the warmest heart,
Yet kindred, comrades, lovers, friends,
Are fated all to part.

The Parting Hour

The one who goes is happier
Than those he leaves behind.

The Parting Hour

LUCY LARCOM
(1824-1893)

I do not own an inch of land,
But all I see is mine.

A Strip of Blue

If the world seems cold to you,
Kindle fires to warm it!

Three Old Saws

If the world's a vale of tears,
Smile, till rainbows span it!

Three Old Saws

There is light in shadow and shadow in light,
And black in the blue of the sky.

Black in Blue Sky. Stanza 2

THOMAS HENRY HUXLEY
(1825-1895)

The chess-board is the world, the pieces are the phenomena of the universe, the rules of the game are what we call the laws of Nature. The player on the other side is hidden from us. We know that his play is always fair, just, and patient. But also we know, to our cost, that he never overlooks a mistake, or makes the smallest allowance for ignorance.

A Liberal Education

Size is not grandeur, and territory does not make a nation.

On University Education (1876)

The great end of life is not knowledge but action.

Technical Education (1877)

STEPHEN COLLINS FOSTER
(1826-1864)

I'm coming, I'm coming, for my head is bending low;
I hear those gentle voices calling, "Old Black Joe."

Old Black Joe. Stanza 3

O, Susanna! O, don't you cry for me,
I've come from Alabama, wid my banjo on my knee.

O, Susanna. Chorus

I dream of Jeanie with the light brown hair,
Borne like a vapor on the summer air;
I see her tripping where the bright streams play,
Happy as the daisies that dance on her way.

Jeanie with the Light Brown Hair
Stanza I

GEORGE MEREDITH
(1828-1913)

I expect that Woman will be the last thing civilized by Man.
The Ordeal of Richard Feverel
(1859) Chap. 1

Who rises from prayer a better man, his prayer is answered.
The Ordeal of Richard Feverel
(1859) Chap. 12

Life is but the pebble sunk;
Deeds, the circle growing!
The Head of Bran the Blest
(1860) IV, Stanza 4

The actors are, it seems, the usual three:
Husband, and wife, and lover.
Modern Love (1862) XXV

That rarest gift
To Beauty, Common Sense.
Modern Love. XXXII

How many a thing which we cast to the ground,
When others pick it up becomes a gem.
Modern Love. XLI

Enter these enchanted woods,
You who dare.
The Woods of Westermain
(1883) Stanza I

She whom I love is hard to catch and conquer,
Hard, but O the glory of the winning were she won!
Love in the Valley (1883)
Stanza 2

HENRIK IBSEN
(1828-1906)

A lie, turned topsy-turvy, can be prinked and tinseled out, decked in plumage new and fine, till none knows its lean old carcass.
Peer Gynt (1867) Act I

For fortune such as I've enjoyed I have to thank America. My amply furnished library I owe to Germany's later schools. From France, again, I get my waistcoats, my manners, and my spice of wit—from England an industrious hand, and keen sense for my own advantage. The Jew has taught me how to wait. Some taste for *dolce far niente* I have received from Italy—and one time, in a perilous pass, to eke the measure of my days, I had recourse to Swedish steel.

Peer Gynt (1867) Act IV

Marriage is a thing you've got to give your whole mind to.

The League of Youth (1869) Act IV

These heroes of finance are like beads on a string—when one slips off, all the rest follow.

The League of Youth (1869) Act IV

Look into any man's heart you please, and you will always find, in every one, at least one black spot which he has to keep concealed.

Pillars of Society (1877) Act III

It is not only what we have inherited from our fathers that exists again in us, but all sorts of old dead ideas and all kinds of old dead beliefs and things of that kind. They are not actually alive in us; but there they are dormant, all the same, and we can never be rid of them. Whenever I take up a newspaper and read it, I fancy I see ghosts creeping between the lines. There must be ghosts all over the world.

Ghosts (1881) Act II

The most crying need in the humbler ranks of life is that they should be allowed some part in the direction of public affairs. That is what will develop their faculties and intelligence and self-respect.

An Enemy of the People (1882)
Act I

The most dangerous enemy to truth and freedom among us is the compact majority.

An Enemy of the People. Act IV

You should never wear your best trousers when you go out to fight for freedom and truth.

An Enemy of the People. Act IV

COUNT LYOF NIKOLAYEVITCH TOLSTOI
((1828-1910)

The Frenchman is conceited from supposing himself mentally and physically to be inordinately fascinating both to men and to women. An Englishman is conceited on the ground of being a citizen of the best-constituted state in the world, and also because he as an Englishman always knows what is the correct thing to do, and knows that everything that he, as an Englishman, does do is indisputably the correct thing. An Italian is conceited from being excitable and easily forgetting himself and other people. A Russian is conceited precisely because he knows nothing and cares to know nothing, since he does not believe it possible to know anything fully. A conceited German is the worst of them all, and the most hardened of all, and the most repulsive of all; for he imagines that he possesses the truth in a science of his own invention, which is to him absolute truth.

War and Peace (1865-1872)
Part IX, Chap. 10

The most powerful weapon of ignorance—the diffusion of printed matter.

War and Peace. Epilogue,
Part II, Chap. 8

All happy families resemble one another; every unhappy family is unhappy in its own fashion.

Anna Karenina (1875-1876)
Part I, Chap. I

The more is given the less the people will work for themselves, and the less they work the more their poverty will increase.

Help for the Starving. Part II
(January, 1892)

CARL SCHURZ
(1829-1906)

Ideals are like stars; you will not succeed in touching them with your hands. But like the seafaring man on the desert of waters, you choose them as your guides, and following them you will reach your destiny.

Help for the Starving
Address, Faneuil Hall, Boston
(April 18, 1859)

Our country, right or wrong. When right, to be kept right; when wrong, to be put right.

Address, Anti-Imperialistic
Conference, Chicago (October 17, 1899)

CHARLES DUDLEY WARNER
(1829-1900)

To own a bit of ground, to scratch it with a hoe, to plant seeds, and watch the renewal of life,—this is the commonest delight of the race, the most satisfactory thing a man can do.

My Summer in a Garden (1870)
Preliminary

True it is that politics makes strange bedfellows.

My Summer in a Garden
Fifteenth Week

Public opinion is stronger than the legislature, and nearly as strong as the ten commandments.

My Summer in a Garden
Sixteenth Week

EMILY DICKINSON
(1830-1886)

If I can stop one heart from breaking,
I shall not live in vain;
If I can ease one life the aching,
Or cool one pain,
Or help one fainting robin
Unto his nest again,
I shall not live in vain.

Part I, Life VI

The soul selects her own society,
Then shuts the door.

Part I, Life XIII, Stanza I